Cables

Volume 1: The Basics

Betty – may all your cables cross the right way!

Janet Szabo

9-5-07

Cables

Volume 1: The Basics

by Janet Szabo

Big Sky Knitting Designs

Photographs and illustrations by Big Sky Knitting Designs
Cover photography by Karen Weyer Photography, Kalispell, MT
Cover design by Teresa Sales, Caldwell, ID

© 2007 Janet Szabo
Big Sky Knitting Designs
3720 Foothill Road
Kalispell, MT 59901

All Rights Reserved

Printed in the United States of America

ISBN 978-0-9768025-1-8

All charts created using Knitter's Symbol Fonts, copyrighted shareware from XRX, Inc.

Table of Contents

Preface

I've discovered that books are like potato chips: it's impossible for me to write just one. In fact, I recently found myself admitting to a friend that I enjoy the process of creating a book almost as much as I enjoy the process of creating a sweater. The two are very similar.

I'm often asked if concentrating on cables ever feels limiting. Wouldn't I like to design lace, or entrelac, or intarsia? Honestly?—no. After all, cables are so versatile that they if I ever want to design in one of those other areas, I can—and I can do it with cables!

My father was fond of saying, "Anything worth doing is worth doing in excess." He was right. Cables (for me, at least) *are* worth doing in excess. To that end, you are holding the first volume of what I plan to be a series of books on cabling techniques. Perhaps you'll never love cables as much as I do, but if you need guidance on knitting them, I want you to find the answers in this book (and the ones to come).

May your cables always cross the right way.

Acknowledgements

Although my name is on the cover, producing a book like this is never a solo endeavor. Thanks go first to JC Briar—in theory, she is the technical editor of the book, but in reality she is also cheerleader, mother confessor, and provider of much-needed sanity checks and appropriate moments of humor. Thinking about writing a book without her input makes me feel faint.

The many charts you find in this book would not be possible were it not for the creative genius of David Xenakis at XRX, Inc. In 1995, I purchased a floppy disk containing the Knitters Symbol Fonts from David at one of the first Stitches events. Those fonts have been the basis of all the charts I've ever produced in my books and newsletter. David has graciously supported my efforts in using and expanding the collection of cable symbols.

Karen Weyer did the cover photography for this book, as she did for *Aran Sweater Design*. Karen has the useful ability to read my mind, and knows just what I am looking for when I say, "Can we do something interesting with this piece of knitting?" Photo shoots with Karen are lots of fun.

Teresa Sales, of The Caxton Printers in Boise, ID, took Karen's photo and created another stunning cover (as she also did for *Aran Sweater Design*). Teresa has been a joy to work with throughout the process of taking my books from computer file to finished objects. I thank her and the crew at Caxton's for their quality work.

I did the index for *Aran Sweater Design*, and it only takes making an index once to know that I am not the right person for that job. Sonya Dintaman stepped in and did a fine job indexing this book.

And of course, I have to thank the three people I live with. They are last on this list, but will always be the first ones I think about when I start my day. First, my husband: Twenty-some years ago when we were in college, I instituted a rule that we could not read anything the other one had written. That was mostly self-preservation on my part. He was the newspaper editor. If I let him read something I had written, it invariably came back covered in red ink. So although he doesn't read my works-in-progress, he listens patiently when I vent about how uncooperative cables are and how they insist that this book be bigger than I intended it to be. I hope he knows how much I appreciate him and his support.

And, my girls: I could not ask for two better children. They are wonderful to have around and I enjoy them more and more every day. I would like my girls to have the gift that my parents gave me—that of finding something in life to be passionate about and making a living from it. They probably won't knit for a living, but I know that they are even now beginning the process of finding that which makes them happy and fulfilled.

How to Use This Book

Cables are the peripatetic stitches of the knitting world. Not content to stay in one place, they travel here, they travel there, and along the way, they see some pretty interesting sights. It was the theme of travel that became the basis for this book. I wanted to write a book on cabling techniques, but needed a way to approach it so that it wasn't just another stitch dictionary. As my technical editor, JC Briar, and I tossed around ideas, she suggested the idea of a travel guide. "Write a book," she said, "focused on how to explore cable patterns. Make it a sort of travel guide full of tips for wandering the Land of Cables."

Here, then, is your guide to the Land of Cables. It's a big country, and this book is hopefully only the first of a series which will guide you through the popular tourist sites as well as lead you to those off-the-beaten-path locations. Like any good travel guide, this book contains suggestions for all kinds of adventurers. Use it in one of the following ways:

1. As a stitch dictionary: This book contains over 100 stitch patterns in written and charted format. Many are favorites of mine, gleaned from years of designing with cables. Some are inventions of my own, which grew out of the process of organizing and categorizing cable stitches for this book. No matter where they came from, all the stitch patterns in this book have something to add to the discussion. Listen to what they have to say.

2. As a visual reference: We've all been dumbfounded—at one time or another—attempting to decipher written instructions for a knitting technique. What exactly does "skip first st and k second st through back of loop" mean? This language can be especially frustrating for newbie knitters. For that reason, I felt it was important to include clear, detailed photos of each and every cabling technique included in this book. Some are common and easily remembered. Others are quite esoteric and you may find yourself looking them up more than once.

3. As an idea book: I wouldn't write books on how to do things if I didn't expect people to go and do those very things I write about. One cannot travel the Land of Cables for long without wanting to "go native." Take the ideas presented here and make them your own. Run with them. Create new cable stitches. The world of knitting will be all the richer for your contribution, whatever it may be.

Developing an itinerary for the journey through the Land of Cables was a definite challenge. Existing stitch dictionaries often divide cable patterns by row repeats, by style (*e.g.*, braids, diamonds) or by use. I finally settled on the system that made the most sense to me. The book is divided into chapters based on the number of stitches in the cable: two-stitch crosses, three-stitch crosses, *etc.* By organizing the book in this way, I was able to present a mostly-linear progression of cables from the simplest two-stitch crosses to complicated crosses involving many stitches.

I also felt it was important to give some background information for each stitch pattern. As a child, I was often teased about reading the dictionary; as a knitting professional, Barbara Walker's stitch dictionaries are some of my favorite bedtime stories. I like to know how a stitch pattern evolved, how it might be used, and how it might be changed and adapted for other situations.

You'll notice that each cable stitch pattern is given in both written and charted format. I personally prefer charts, although it took me a long time to become comfortable using them. If you want to design any original cable patterns—or tweak existing ones—the process is much easier when you have a visual representation in front of you. As you use this book as a stitch dictionary, you will begin to see the relationships between the various groups of cables, and how one cable gives birth to another just by adding or changing some of the elements.

My hope is that you will enjoy traveling the Land of Cables, because there is so much to see and do. Take your time, explore, get to know the locals, and above all, have fun.

Chapter 1

Fundamentals

Preparing for a trip ahead of time helps to insure that everything will go smoothly. Knitting is no different. Let's get ready for our trip through the Land of Cables by taking some time to review the basics of cable knitting: yarns, needles, a bit about the language, and what to do if something goes wrong. Here is where you will also find the list of abbreviations and key to symbols used throughout the book.

Yarn Construction

I became a much better knitter when I learned to spin my own yarns. Suddenly forced to make choices in the construction of a yarn—fuzzy or smooth? singles or plied?—I also had to take a hard look at what the yarn was used for. Not all yarns are suitable for all projects. It might seem an obvious truth, but it's overlooked by a lot of knitters.

Unless you are also a spinner as well as a knitter, you're probably not aware of the differences in yarns. You might recognize that some yarns aren't suitable for certain projects, but you don't know exactly why. Think about what draws you to a yarn—for example, when you walk in to a yarn store, why do you gravitate to a particular yarn? For most of us, it's the color. We're immediately drawn to a yarn because it's red, or blue, or that elusive shade of chartreuse we've been searching for. Only after we pick up a yarn do we notice that it's soft, or harsh, or smooth, or hairy. Aside from the cable patterns in a design, the construction of the yarn has the biggest impact on the final look of a cabled project.

Let's take a few moments and examine how yarn construction affects the appearance of cables, and how you can become a savvy cable-knitting yarn consumer.

Woolen- vs. Worsted-Spun Yarns

Yarns can be divided broadly into two categories: woolen-spun and worsted-spun. Note—and this is very important—that "woolen" used in this context refers to the construction of a yarn, not the fiber content. Woolen-spun yarns can be spun from wool, cotton, cashmere, and many other fibers. Note also that "worsted" used in this context refers to the construction of the yarn, not the weight. Worsted-spun yarns can range from fingering weight to bulky weight.

For purposes of this discussion, "woolen-spun" and "worsted-spun" will comprise the two ends of a yarn continuum. In between are many "semi-woolen" and "semi-worsted" yarns—yarns which have characteristics of both woolen-spun and worsted-spun construction. Once you recognize the differences between these yarns, you'll be better able to make educated decisions about what yarn to use for a project.

Woolen-Spun Yarns	Worsted-Spun Yarns
They are spun from shorter fibers, from 1" to 2" in length. Sheep breeds that produce these shorter fibers are Merino, Columbia, Targhee, and Shetland.	They are spun from long fibers, anything from 4" to 11" in length. Sheep breeds that produce these longer fibers include Lincoln, Cotswold, Wensleydale, Bluefaced Leicester, and other "longwool" breeds.
Wool fibers used in woolen-spun yarns tend to be very crimpy or wavy.	The fibers are generally straight or slightly wavy, and may have a shiny surface that reflects light.
The fibers are carded before spinning, which produces a web of randomly-arranged fibers of varying lengths.	The fibers are combed before spinning to remove short fibers and vegetable matter. The fibers which are left are uniform in length and are parallel to one another.
The spinning method preserves the loftiness and elasticity of the fibers; woolen-spun yarns do not have as much twist as worsted-spun yarns, making them feel less harsh against the skin.	The spinning method preserves the fibers' parallel arrangement. Worsted-spun yarns contain a lot of twist.
A woolen-spun yarn is not as durable as a worsted-spun yarn because it has a greater tendency to pill.	The surface of the yarn is smooth, durable, and long-wearing. Worsted-spun yarns are the least likely yarns to pill.
A woolen-spun yarn has better insulating qualities than a worsted-spun yarn.	Because very little air is trapped within the fibers during spinning, worsted-spun yarns are not very insulating.

You may ask, "Which yarn is the better choice for a cabled project?" The answer is, "It depends." Much depends upon the result you, the knitter, are looking for. If you want to showcase your knitting talents with complicated cable patterning, a worsted-spun yarn will likely show it off to better advantage. If, however, you want a sweater in which the cables have a softer, more muted appearance, choose a woolen-spun yarn. Swatching is the best way to determine if a particular yarn is suitable for a project.

Plies and Stitch Definition

Another factor in the choice of yarns for a cabled project is the number of plies in a yarn. Note that some knitters (those outside of the U.S. and those who have been knitting for 50 or 60 years) may be more familiar with "ply" as a designation for weight, *e.g.*, a 2-ply is thinner than a 4-ply or an 8-ply. Here, "ply" refers to the number of individual strands making up a multi-ply yarn.

A singles yarn will give adequate stitch definition, but has the unfortunate tendency to "bias" or slant on the diagonal. This is because the process of adding twist to the fibers adds energy to the strand of yarn that is not balanced out by another strand of yarn. The twist energy makes itself apparent in the slant of the fabric. This is not to say that singles yarns are unsuitable, simply that they need to be spun loosely enough so that the bias is less apparent. Beware of singles yarns that are so tightly twisted that they kink up on themselves.

A 2-ply yarn is the favorite of handspinners anxious to complete the spinning process and begin knitting with their yarn. A 2-ply yarn is created by twisting two strands of yarns together in the direction opposite of that in which they were spun. Plying a yarn balances out its twist and makes it less likely to bias. Plying also makes the yarn thicker than the individual plies composing it.

Plying more than two strands of yarn together yields yarns which not only increase in diameter, but have a rounder cross-section, as well (see Figure 1).

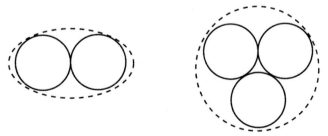

Fig. 1, L to R: *Cross-section of a 2-ply yarn, cross-section of a 3-ply yarn.*

This rounder cross-section provides a subtle improvement in stitch definition. As a spinner and knitter, I concluded that this improvement was enough to justify the extra work it takes to create a 3-, 4-, or 5-ply yarn instead of just a 2-ply yarn.

Needles

Needle preferences are very personal, and each knitter needs to find those needles which are most comfortable for him or her. For instance, I don't like to use the nickel-plated knitting needles. They are too slippery for me; I find myself clutching the yarn and needles which eventually makes my hands cramp up. I much prefer the coated aluminum needles, but even within that category I have a preference for needles with very sharp tips. Sharp-tipped needles make working some cabling maneuvers much easier. Some knitters may prefer wood or bamboo. Much depends upon the type of fiber you are using and the way you knit. Experiment until you find those needles which are most comfortable for you to use.

Cable Needles

Cable needles come in a variety of shapes and sizes. Thin aluminum-coated glove needles (about 4" long) work well. Novice cablers may prefer to use shaped ones as the stitches are less likely to fall off the needle. Wooden ones are good to use when working with a slippery yarn like a slick cotton or rayon.

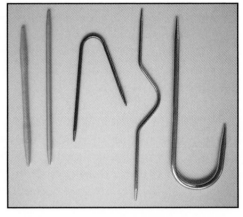

Fig. 2: *A variety of cable needles. From L to R: Straight wooden, straight aluminum-coated, U-shaped, gull-wing shaped, and J-shaped.*

Cabling Without a Cable Needle

Many knitters learn to cable without a cable needle, which increases knitting speed and eliminates an extra tool. In some situations, however—such as when knitting with slippery yarn, or an inelastic yarn, or if the cable is complicated—a cable needle is as essential as knitting needles.

Shown on the next page is a 3-stitch-over-3-stitch right cross made without a cable needle.

Cabling Without a Cable Needle

1. Slip the stitches of the cable off the left-hand needle

2. Insert the right-hand needle into the three stitches at the far left of the cable.

3. Take the left-hand needle behind the work and insert it into the remaining three stitches.

4. Slip the three stitches from the right-hand needle back to the left-hand needle. The stitches have been crossed.

5. Knit all stitches of the cable from the left-hand needle.

Cable Nomenclature

As with many other aspects of knitting, there is no single universal method of describing cables in written knitting patterns. Barbara Walker uses one system in her *Treasuries*, the Harmony series of stitch pattern books uses another system, and still other naming systems are used by magazines and in computer software. The following table illustrates just how confusing it can be when the same cable is classified differently by different naming systems:

Cable Maneuver	Walker's *Treasuries*	Harmony Stitch Guides	*Knitter's* Magazine
Slip next stitch to cable needle and hold at back of work, k2, k1 from cable needle	BC: Back Cross	C3B: Cable 3 Back	2/1 RC (2/1 Right Cross)
Slip next 2 sts to cable needle and hold at front of work, p1, k2 from cable needle	FC: Front Cross	T3B: Twist 3 Front	2/1 LPC (2/1 Left Purl Cross)
Slip next 2 sts to cable needle and hold at back of work, k2, k2 from cable needle	BKC: Back Knit Cross	C4B: Cable 4 Back	2/2 RC (2/2 Right Cross)
Slip next 2 sts to cable needle and hold at front of work, p2, k2 from cable needle	FC: Front Cross	T4F: Twist 4 Front	2/2 LPC (2/2 Left Purl Cross)

I don't care for Barbara Walker's cable abbreviations because she uses the same abbreviation (*e.g.*, FC for Front Cross) to describe more than one cable manuever. For example, in *A Second Treasury of Knitting Patterns*, the abbreviation FC in the Telescope Lattice pattern means "slip 2 stitches to cable needle and hold in front, k2, then k2 from cable needle." In the Rib and Braid pattern, FC means "slip 1 stitch to cable needle and hold at front of work, p1, then k1 from cable needle." Just when you think you have the definition of FC memorized, it changes!

The abbreviations used in the Harmony stitch books are more consistent, but still do not describe adequately the cable crossing maneuvers.

My favorite cable naming system is the one used by *Knitter's* Magazine and by other contemporary knitting publications. It not only indicates which way the cable crosses (R or L), it specifies how many stitches cross over how many stitches, and what stitch maneuvers (knit or purl) are involved. Look at these examples:

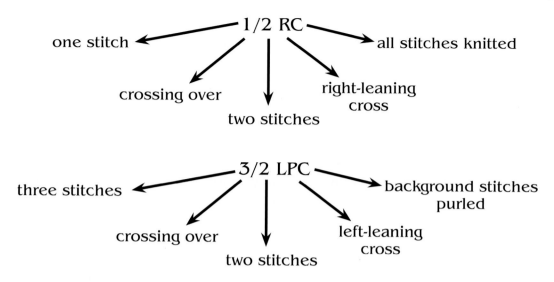

Whenever the instructions include an "R" it means that the cable leans to the right and the stitches on the cable needle should be held at the back of the work. When the instructions include an "L" it means that the cable leans to the left and the stitches on the cable needle should be held at the front of the work. If the instructions include a "P" it means that some of the stitches in the crossing should be purled. However, even this much descriptive information does not eliminate the need for a comprehensive list of abbreviations and what they mean; it simply makes it easier to understand each abbreviation within the body of the pattern.

If you're using several cable patterns in a design, and they come from different stitch pattern books using different naming systems, it's best to pick one system and use it for all the cable patterns in your design. That is especially important if you are writing down your instructions for other knitters to follow.

Most cables also have fanciful common names (*e.g.*, Aran Honeycomb, Ladder of Life, *etc.*) which are somewhat descriptive, but do not describe how the cable is knitted. To further muddy the waters, the same cable pattern may be known by different common names, depending upon the source.

Cable Charts

I strongly recommend working from charts whenever possible. Some knitters insist that they cannot work from charts and can only work from written instructions. I understand, because I used to be one of those knitters. It takes a bit of practice, but I believe everyone can learn to work from charts. It's much like learning to read a map.

Perhaps the most important reason for working from charts is that a chart gives an immediate visual confirmation of the pattern. Compare the knitted fabric to the chart and see instantly if there is an error. Becoming comfortable with a visual representation of the knitted fabric also leads to less reliance on charts or written instructions—it becomes easier to "read" the knitting and anticipate the next cable crossing. And if you have any desire at all to design original cable patterns, learning to work from charts is an essential skill!

A number of different sets of knitting symbols are currently in use, and all differ slightly. Knitters who draw their charts by hand can use whichever set of symbols they like. (I recommend the set Barbara Walker uses in *Charted Knitting Designs.*) Commercial charting software is available, but the programs and capabilities differ widely.

Graph paper is useful for charting out cable stitch patterns—either ones you plan to use in a design (if you don't have computer-generated charts), or for designing your own original stitch patterns. Even though I use computer-generated charts for most of my designs, I find creating new stitch patterns from scratch to be easier with some graph paper, a sharp pencil, and an eraser. Either regular graph paper or knitter's graph paper is suitable, although the latter will give you a better indication of how the stitch will look knitted up.

Cable Splay

"Cable splay" is a phenomenon that occurs at the transition of a cable pattern into another stitch pattern, such as ribbing. The gauges of the two stitch patterns differ to such an extent that the fabric is distorted.

The swatch in Figure 3 illustrates this problem. Notice that at the point where the seed stitch border ends and the cable begins, the cable "splays" out, distorting the bottom edge of the swatch. The top edge of the swatch, where the cable transitions into the seed stitch border, is also distorted. This phenomenon can happen whenever there is a transition from one pattern (*e.g.*, ribbing, stockinette, seed stitch) into a cable pattern. Some cable patterns suffer from this problem more than others (you'll be able to tell from your swatch). You can compensate for it in one or both of two ways:

1. Increase at the base of any cable wider than four stitches. How many increases should you make? An increase stitch or two at the base of each cable crossing should eliminate the problem. When you reach the other end of the piece, make the corresponding decrease(s).

Fig. 3: *Cable splay.*

2. Make sure there is a cable crossing on the first or second right-side row after beginning the cable pattern, and another just before ending the cable. This is a good practice to follow even when cable splay isn't an issue, as it looks more polished.

Figure 4 shows a swatch where cable splay has been minimized using both of the methods discussed above.

Fig. 4: *Adjusting for cable splay with increases and decreases at the transition points, and with cable crosses at the beginning and end of the cable.*

Fixing Mistakes

It's a terrible feeling to get halfway up the body of a sweater and realize that there is a mistake 3" back. Get into the habit of checking your work frequently. That way, if a mistake needs to be fixed, it will be less complicated to do so.

Don't panic if a mistake in the cabling makes itself known. It's likely possible to fix just that cable. I use one of two methods depending upon the location of the cable. If the mistake is only a few rows back, simply drop down the stitches of the cable and re-knit them in their proper positions (see photos, below). If the cable needing repair is a simple vertical one which doesn't travel over background stitches, you may elect to drop down only half of the stitches—e.g., drop down the half that ought to be in front but are in back, bring them to the front, then knit them back up.

1. Drop the stitches of the mis-crossed cable off the left-hand needle.

2. Ladder the dropped stitches just beyond the mis-crossed row. Place them on a needle.

3. Orient the stitches for the cable in their proper positions.

4. Using the strands of yarn that were pulled out of the laddered-down stitches, reknit the cable.

5. Reknit the rows following the cable.

6. Place the corrected cable back onto the left-hand needle and continue with the work.

Sometimes, however, a mistake isn't obvious until after the sweater has been completed, or work has progressed beyond a point where it would be practical to ladder down the stitches and fix the cable. Or perhaps the mistake is part of a very complex cable panel and too wide a section of knitting would have to be laddered down and reknit. In these cases, it's possible—with a little creative surgery—to snip the top half of the cross, move it behind the rest of the cross, then rejoin the stitches. The following photos illustrate how it's done. If you need to use this method, practice on a swatch, first!

1. Identify the row above and below the cable cross (hint: the cabled row is not "connected" to the base fabric and can be lifted up). Run contrasting yarn through those stitches.

2. Snip the middle stitch of the row between the marking threads. Carefully unravel that strand of yarn to either side.

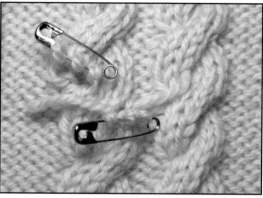

3. Place the stitches that were held by the marking threads on small safety pins. Notice the short strands of yarn that were unraveled in Step 2.

4. Bring the safety pins holding the live stitches to the back of the work. Transfer the stitches to short double-pointed needles. Graft the live stitches together.

5. Darn in the ends of the snipped yarn and the repair yarn. Admire your work!

Abbreviations and key to charts

The charts in this book were generated using Knitters Symbol Fonts from XRX, Inc. This font can be used in any word processing program. The basic set contains symbols for cables involving up to four stitches. For cables involving more than four stitches, or for cables which require additional maneuvers, I have created my own symbols based on the conventions given in the original font.

For each group of symbols, the right cross symbol (all stitches knitted) and its abbreviation and description are given first, followed by the same information for the left cross. If there is a cross for that group involving purl stitches, it follows next, and the symbol is shaded.

│	Knit on RS, purl on WS
─	Purl on RS, knit on WS
ɣ	K1tbl (Knit 1 through back loop): Knit into back of st on RS, purl into back of st on WS
O	Yarn over
K	MK (Make Knot): (K1, p1, k1, p1, k1) into next st, then, with the point of the LH needle, pass the 2nd, 3rd, 4th, and 5th st on RH needle over the 1st st
/	K2tog
\	SSK
⋏	Sl2—k1—p2sso: Slip the next 2 sts as if to k2tog, k1, then pass the 2 slipped sts over

Two-Stitch Crosses

 1/1 RC (1/1 Right Cross)

On RS of work: Slip next st to cable needle and hold at back of work, k1, then k st from cable needle

On WS of work: Bring RH needle in front of first st on LH needle and purl second st, then purl the first stitch, then drop both from LH needle

1/1 LC (1/1 Left Cross)

On RS of work: Slip next st to cable needle and hold at front of work, k1, then k st from cable needle

On WS of work: Slip 2 sts one at a time as if to knit, then return them to the LH needle in the turned position. Purl them together through the backs of the loops, then purl the first st again through the back of its loop. Drop both sts from LH needle together.

1/1 RPC (1/1 Right Purl Cross): Slip next st to cable needle and hold at back of work, k1, then p1 from cable needle

1/1 LPC (1/1 Left Purl Cross): Slip next st to cable needle and hold at front of work, p1, then k1 from cable needle

Three-Stitch Crosses

1/2 RC (1/2 Right Cross): Slip next 2 sts to cable needle and hold at back of work, k1, then k2 from cable needle

1/2 LC (1/2 Left Cross): Slip next st to cable needle and hold at front of work, k2, then k1 from cable needle

1/2 RPC (1/2 Right Purl Cross): Slip next 2 sts to cable needle and hold at back of work, k1, then p2 from cable needle

1/2 LPC (1/2 Left Purl Cross): Slip next st to cable needle and hold at front of work, p2, then k1 from cable needle

2/1 RC (2/1 Right Cross): Slip next st to cable needle and hold at back of work, k2, then k1 from cable needle

2/1 LC (2/1 Left Cross): Slip next 2 sts to cable needle and hold at front of work, k1, then k2 from cable needle

2/1 RPC (2/1 Right Purl Cross): Slip next st to cable needle and hold at back of work, k2, then p1 from cable needle

2/1 LPC (2/1 Left Purl Cross): Slip next 2 sts to cable needle and hold at front of work, p1, then k2 from cable needle

1/1/1 RC (1/1/1 Right Cross): Slip next 2 sts to cable needle and hold at back of work, k1, slip left-most st from cable needle back to LH needle and knit it, then k1 from cable needle

1/1/1 LC (1/1/1 Left Cross): Slip next 2 sts to cable needle and hold at front of work, k1, slip left-most st from cable needle back to LH needle and knit it, then k1 from cable needle

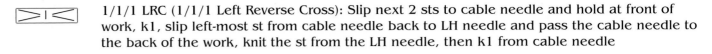 1/1/1 LRC (1/1/1 Left Reverse Cross): Slip next 2 sts to cable needle and hold at front of work, k1, slip left-most st from cable needle back to LH needle and pass the cable needle to the back of the work, knit the st from the LH needle, then k1 from cable needle

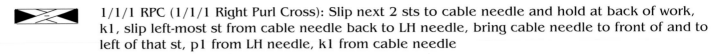 1/1/1 RPC (1/1/1 Right Purl Cross): Slip next 2 sts to cable needle and hold at back of work, k1, slip left-most st from cable needle back to LH needle, bring cable needle to front of and to left of that st, p1 from LH needle, k1 from cable needle

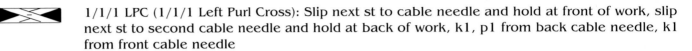 1/1/1 LPC (1/1/1 Left Purl Cross): Slip next st to cable needle and hold at front of work, slip next st to second cable needle and hold at back of work, k1, p1 from back cable needle, k1 from front cable needle

Four-Stitch Crosses

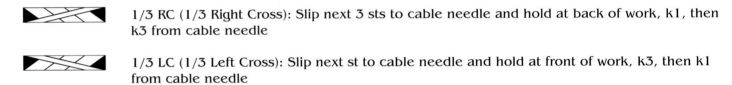 1/3 RC (1/3 Right Cross): Slip next 3 sts to cable needle and hold at back of work, k1, then k3 from cable needle

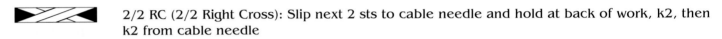 1/3 LC (1/3 Left Cross): Slip next st to cable needle and hold at front of work, k3, then k1 from cable needle

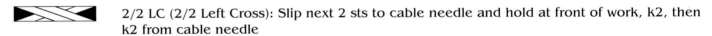 2/2 RC (2/2 Right Cross): Slip next 2 sts to cable needle and hold at back of work, k2, then k2 from cable needle

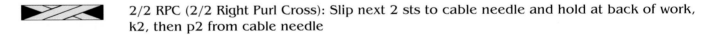 2/2 LC (2/2 Left Cross): Slip next 2 sts to cable needle and hold at front of work, k2, then k2 from cable needle

2/2 RPC (2/2 Right Purl Cross): Slip next 2 sts to cable needle and hold at back of work, k2, then p2 from cable needle

2/2 LPC (2/2 Left Purl Cross): Slip next 2 sts to cable needle and hold at front of work, p2, then k2 from cable needle

3/1 RC (3/1 Right Cross): Slip next st to cable needle and hold at back of work, k3, then k1 from cable needle

3/1 LC (3/1 Left Cross): Slip next 3 sts to cable needle and hold at front of work, k1, then k3 from cable needle

3/1 RPC (3/1 Right Cross): Slip next st to cable needle and hold at back of work, k3, then p1 from cable needle

3/1 LPC (3/1 Left Cross): Slip next 3 sts to cable needle and hold at front of work, p1, then k3 from cable needle

1/2/1 RC (1/2/1 Right Cross): Slip next 3 sts to cable needle and hold at back of work, k1, slip 2 left-most sts from cable needle back to LH needle and knit them, then k1 from cable needle

1/2/1 LC (1/2/1 Left Cross): Slip next 3 sts to cable needle and hold at front of work, k1, slip 2 left-most sts from cable needle back to LH needle and knit them, then k1 from cable needle

1/2/1 RPC (1/2/1 Right Purl Cross): Slip next 3 sts to cable needle and hold at back of work, k1, slip 2 left-most sts from cable needle back to LH needle, bring the cable needle to the front of and to the left of those sts, p2 from LH needle, k1 from cable needle

1/2/1 LPC (1/2/1 Left Purl Cross): Slip next st to cable needle and hold at front of work, slip next 2 sts to a second cable needle and hold at back of work, k1, p2 from back cable needle, k1 from front cable needle

Five-Stitch Crosses

2/3 RC (2/3 Right Cross): Slip next 3 sts to cable needle and hold at back of work, k2, then k3 from cable needle

2/3 LC (2/3 Left Cross): Slip next 2 sts to cable needle and hold at front of work, k3, then k2 from cable needle

2/3 RPC (2/3 Right Purl Cross): Slip next 3 sts to cable needle and hold at back of work, k2, then p3 from cable needle

2/3 LPC (2/3 Left Purl Cross): Slip next 2 sts to cable needle and hold at front of work, p3, then k2 from cable needle

3/2 RC (3/2 Right Cross): Slip next 2 sts to cable needle and hold at back of work, k3, then k2 from cable needle

3/2 LC (3/2 Left Cross): Slip next 3 sts to cable needle and hold at front of work, k2, then k3 from cable needle

3/2 RPC (3/2 Right Purl Cross): Slip next 2 sts to cable needle and hold at back of work, k3, then p2 from cable needle

3/2 LPC (3/2 Left Purl Cross): Slip next 3 sts to cable needle and hold at front of work, p2, then k3 from cable needle

1/3/1 RC (1/3/1 Right Cross): Slip next four sts to cable needle and hold at back of work, k1, slip 3 left-most sts from cable needle back to LH needle and knit them, then k1 from cable needle

1/3/1 LC (1/3/1 Left Cross): Slip next four sts to cable needle and hold at front of work, k1, slip 3 left-most sts from cable needle back to LH needle and knit them, then k1 from cable needle

2/1/2 RC (2/1/2 Right Cross): Slip next 3 sts to cable needle and hold at back of work, k2, slip left-most st from cable needle back to LH needle and knit it, then k2 from cable needle

2/1/2 LC (2/1/2 Left Cross): Slip next 3 sts to cable needle and hold at front of work, k2, slip left-most st from cable needle back to LH needle and knit it, then k2 from cable needle

2/1/2 RPC (2/1/2 Right Purl Cross): Slip next 3 sts to cable needle and hold at back of work, k2, slip left-most st from cable needle back to LH needle, bring cable needle to the front of and to the left of that st, p1 from LH needle, then k2 from cable needle

2/1/2 LPC (2/1/2 Left Purl Cross): Slip next 2 sts to cable needle and hold at front of work, slip next st to second cable needle and hold at back of work, k2, p1 from back cable needle, k2 from front cable needle

4/1 RC (4/1 Right Cross): Slip next st to cable needle and hold at back of work, k4, then k1 from cable needle

4/1 LC (4/1 Left Cross): Slip next 4 sts to cable needle and hold at front of work, k1, then k4 from cable needle

4/1 RPC (4/1 Right Purl Cross): Slip next st to cable needle and hold at back of work, k4, then p1 from cable needle

4/1 LPC (4/1 Left Purl Cross): Slip next 4 sts to cable needle and hold at front of work, p1, then k4 from cable needle

Six-Stitch Crosses

2/4 RC (2/4 Right Cross): Slip next 4 sts to cable needle and hold at back of work, k2, then k4 from cable needle

2/4 LC (2/4 Left Cross): Slip next 2 sts to cable needle and hold at front of work, k4, then k2 from cable needle

2/4 RPC (2/4 Right Purl Cross): Slip next 4 sts to cable needle and hold at back of work, k2, then p4 from cable needle

2/4 LPC (2/4 Left Purl Cross): Slip next 2 sts to cable needle and hold at front of work, p4, then k2 from cable needle

3/3 RC (3/3 Right Cross): Slip next 3 sts to cable needle and hold at back of work, k3, then k3 from cable needle

3/3 LC (3/3 Left Cross): Slip next 3 sts to cable needle and hold at front of work, k3, then k3 from cable needle

3/3 RPC (3/3 Right Purl Cross): Slip next 3 sts to cable needle and hold at back of work, k3, then p3 from cable needle

3/3 LPC (3/3 Left Purl Cross): Slip next 3 sts to cable needle and hold at front of work, p3, then k3 from cable needle

2/2/2 RC (2/2/2 Right Cross): Slip next 4 sts to cable needle and hold at back of work, k2, then slip 2 left-most sts from cable needle back to LH and pass cable needle to front of work, k2 from LH needle and k2 from cable needle

2/2/2 LC (2/2/2 Left Cross): Slip next 2 sts to cable needle and hold at front of work, slip next 2 sts to second cable needle and hold at back of work, k2, then k2 from back cable needle, then k2 from front cable needle

2/2/2 RRC (2/2/2 Right Reverse Cross): Slip next 2 sts to cable needle and hold at back of work, slip next 2 sts to second cable needle and hold at front of work, k2, then k2 from front cable needle and k2 from back cable needle

2/2/2 LRC (2/2/2 Left Reverse Cross): Slip next 4 sts to cable needle and hold at front of work, k2, then slip left-most 2 sts from cable needle back to LH and pass cable needle to back of work, k2 from LH needle and k2 from cable needle

 2/2/2 RPC (2/2/2 Right Purl Cross): Slip next 4 sts to cable needle and hold at back of work, k2, the slip 2 left-most sts from cable needle back to LH needle and bring cable needle to front of and to left of those sts, p2 from LH needle, k2 from cable needle

 2/2/2 LPC (2/2/2 Left Purl Cross): Slip next 2 sts to cable needle and hold at front of work, slip next 2 sts to second cable needle and hold at back of work, k2, p2 from back cable needle, k2 from front cable needle

Seven-Stitch Crosses

 3/4 RC (3/4 Right Cross): Slip next 4 sts to cable needle and hold at back of work, k3, then k4 from cable needle

 3/4 LC (3/4 Left Cross): Slip next 3 sts to cable needle and hold at front of work, k4, then k3 from cable needle

 3/1/3 RC (3/1/3 Right Cross): Slip next 4 sts to cable needle and hold at back of work, k3, slip left-most st from cable needle back to LH needle and knit it, then k3 from cable needle

 3/1/3 LC (3/1/3 Left Cross): Slip next 4 sts to cable needle and hold at front of work, k3, slip left-most st from cable needle back to LH needle and knit it, then k3 from cable needle

 3/1/3 RPC (3/1/3 Right Purl Cross): Slip next 4 sts to cable needle and hold at back of work, k3, slip left-most st from cable needle back to LH needle and purl it, then k3 from cable needle

 3/1/3 LPC (3/1/3 Left Purl Cross): Slip next 4 sts to cable needle and hold at front of work, k3, slip left-most st from cable needle back to LH needle and purl it, then k3 from cable needle

Eight-Stitch Crosses

 4/4 RC (4/4 Right Cross): Slip next 4 sts to cable needle and hold at back of work, k4, then k4 from cable needle

 4/4 LC (4/4 Left Cross): Slip next 4 sts to cable needle and hold at front of work, k4, then k4 from cable needle

Nine-Stitch Crosses

5/4 RC (5/4 Right Cross): Slip next 4 sts to cable needle and hold at back of work, k5, then k4 from cable needle

5/4 LC (5/4 Left Cross): Slip next 5 sts to cable needle and hold at front of work, k4, then k5 from cable needle

Ten-Stitch Crosses

5/5 RC (5/5 Right Cross): Slip next 5 sts to cable needle and hold at back of work, k5, then k5 from cable needle

5/5 LC (5/5 Left Cross): Slip next 5 sts to cable needle and hold at front of work, k5, then k5 from cable needle

Twelve-Stitch Crosses

6/6 RC (6/6 Right Cross): Slip next 6 sts to cable needle and hold at back of work, k6, then k6 from cable needle

6/6 LC (6/6 Left Cross): Slip next 6 sts to cable needle and hold at front of work, k6, then k6 from cable needle

Two-Stitch Crosses

The most basic form of a cable is two stitches exchanging places with each other. This exchange can happen randomly within a piece of knitted fabric, or in some form of repeating pattern. The stitches exchanging places can be both knits, both purls, or a combination of knit and purl. Once you've mastered these maneuvers, most other crosses are easily understood.

Cables vs. Twists: Some discussion needs to be given here to the difference between *cables* and *twists*. A *cable* is formed by removing a stitch (or group of stitches) from the working space—either by slipping it to a separate needle and holding it away from the fabric, or by dropping it off the working needle to await its turn in the exchange. This act of removing the stitch from the fabric and adding it back later results in a well-defined crossing of stitches.

A *twist*, on the other hand, doesn't require the physical removal of the stitch from the working space. Some deft sleight-of-hand with the yarn and needles results in the stitches exchanging places with each other. These terms are often used interchangeably. Although both techniques yield the same result—stitches moved—there are subtle but important differences between them. Some may argue that it matters not which method is used, but my experience is that it does. Choose whichever method you prefer, but make an *educated* choice.

The difference between cables and twists is more pronounced with the left twists than with the right twists. The next time you work a left twist in a pattern, notice the path that the yarn travels: it must go behind the first stitch (the skipped one), make the second stitch, then go back and make the first stitch. That extra length of yarn causes the twist to "hump up" from the surface of the fabric. The difference is more pronounced when left twists are paired with right twists than when left twists are the only crossings in the fabric.

Also, it's quite easy to stretch out the stitches—even unintentionally—when working a left twist. The right-hand needle has to insinuate itself into the backs of stitches. Unless this is done with the stitches close to the tips of the needles, some stretching is inevitable. Despite those considerations, the clear advantage to working twists instead of cables is their speed.

Both cables and twists can be worked on either the public or private side of the fabric. The technique for making cables is the same no matter which side of the fabric is the active side. Twists are worked differently depending upon if they are knitted or purled.

Also included in this chapter are instructions for working knit/purl crosses worked either as cables or as twists.

Note that for simplicity, this book refers to all two-stitch crosses as cables. You are free, however, to work the crosses as either cables or twists, as you choose.

1/1 Knit Crosses, Cable Versions: These are ideal crosses on which to practice cabling without a cable needle.

1/1 Right Cross

1. Slip the next stitch to a cable needle and hold at the back of the work.

2. Knit the next stitch from the left-hand needle.

3. Knit the stitch from the cable needle.

1/1 Left Cross

1. Slip the next stitch to a cable needle and hold at the front of the work.

2. Knit the next stitch from the left-hand needle.

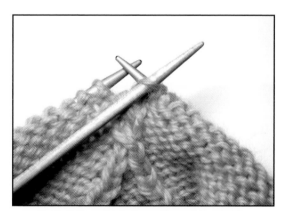

3. Knit the stitch from the cable needle.

1/1 Knit Crosses, Twist Versions: A right knit twist (referred to here simply as "right twist") can be worked in one of two ways. The first has been handed down through generations of knitters; the second is Barbara Walker's "improved" method as outlined in *A Second Treasury of Knitting Patterns.*

1/1 Right Cross, Twist Version 1

1. Bring right-hand needle in front of first stitch, and knit the second stitch.

2. Knit the skipped stitch, and drop both stitches from the needle together.

1/1 Right Cross, Twist Version 2

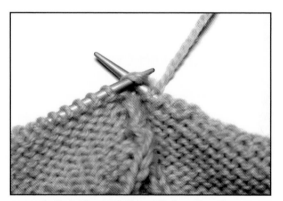

1. Knit the next two stitches together.

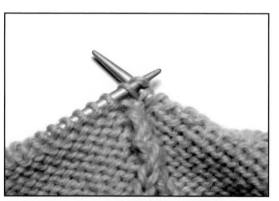

2. Knit the first stitch again, dropping both stitches from the needle together.

The left twist also has two versions, shown below.

1. Bring the right-hand needle behind the first stitch and knit the second stitch through the back of the loop.

2. Knit the skipped stitch in the front of the loop, dropping both stitches from the left-hand needle together.

1/1 Left Cross, Twist Version 1

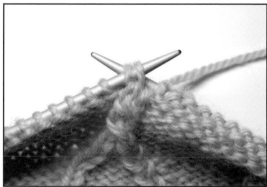

1. Bring the right-hand needle behind the first stitch and knit the second stitch through the back of the loop.

2. Insert the right-hand needle into the backs of both stitches (the skipped stitch and the second stitch), and knit two together through the backs of the loops.

1/1 Left Cross, Twist Version 2

Pattern 2.1: Placing 1/1 right and left crosses randomly, or staggering them across the surface of stockinette stitch, provides a simple accent, and makes a great alternative to plain stockinette stitch.

This stitch pattern is one in which the twist direction of the yarn has much to do with the appearance of the fabric. If the direction of the cable and of the twist of the yarn are the same, the fabric has a flatter appearance than if the direction of the cable and the twist of the yarn are in opposite directions. Swatching with a potential yarn will tell you which appearance you prefer.

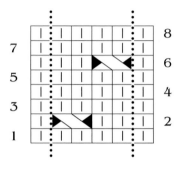

Multiple of 4 stitches + 2

Row 1 and all other WS rows: Purl
Row 2: K1, *k2, 1/1 LC; rep from *, end k1
Rows 4 and 8: Knit
Row 6: K1, *1/1 LC, k2; rep from *, end k1

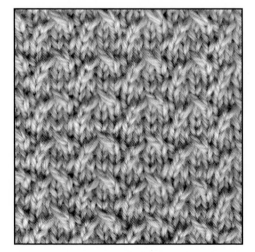

Variation #1: Here, crossings are spaced every other row, and the direction of the cross alternates—a left cross on one right-side row, and a right cross on the following right-side row.

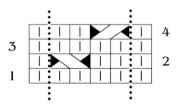

Multiple of 4 stitches + 2

Row 1 and all other WS rows: Purl
Row 2: K1, *k2, 1/1 LC; rep from *, end k1
Row 4: K1, *1/1 RC, k2; rep from *, end k1

Variation #2: This variation shows right and left crosses combining to form an "X" shape.

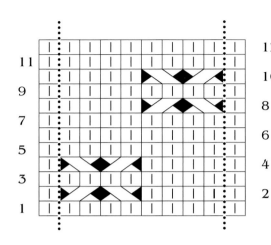

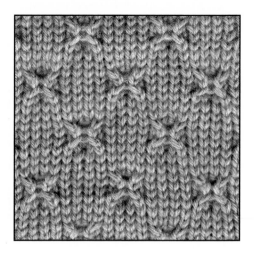

12 Multiple of 8 stitches + 2

10 Row 1 and all other WS rows: Purl
    Row 2: K1, *k4, 1/1 LC, 1/1 RC; rep from *, end k1
 8 Row 4: K1, *k4, 1/1 RC, 1/1 LC; rep from *, end k1
    Rows 6 and 12: Knit
 6
    Row 8: K1, *1/1 LC, 1/1 RC, k4; rep from *, end k1
 4 Row 10: K1, *1/1 RC, 1/1 LC, k4; rep from *, end k1

Ideas for Further Exploration

1. Increase the number of stitches between the cable crosses to make a more widely-scattered cable pattern.

2. Increase or decrease the number of rows between the cable crosses.

3. Add beads—one at the base of each single cross, or one in the center of a combination of crosses.

4. On the row below the cross, knit the crossing stitch(es) in a contrasting color of yarn to provide "spots" of color across the surface of the fabric.

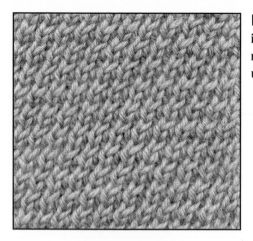

Pattern 2.2: Crossing adjacent pairs of stitches repeatedly across a row of fabric creates a pattern of slanting stitches. Each crossing row alternates with one of plain knitting, and the crossings move to the left or right (depending upon the orientation chosen by the knitter) by one stitch on each crossing row. This is a useful, non-rolling trim pattern when worked at the edges of a sweater.

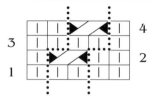

Multiple of 2 stitches + 3

Rows 1 and 3 (WS): Purl
Row 2: K2, *1/1 RC; rep from *, end k1
Row 4: K1, *1/1 RC; rep from *, end k2

Variation #1: Working the pattern over three stitches forms a narrow cable sometimes referred to as a "mock cable."

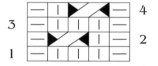

Panel of 5 stitches

Rows 1 and 3 (WS): K1, p3, k1
Row 2: P1, k1, 1/1 RC, p1
Row 4: P1, 1/1 RC, k1, p1

Ideas for Further Exploration

1. Work pattern 2.2 for 10, 12, or more rows using 1/1 right crosses, then switch to 1/1 left crosses for the same number of rows. Continue to alternate in this manner to form a herringbone-style pattern.

2. Repeat the three-stitch cable in Variation 1 over the width of the fabric for an interesting alternative to plain ribbing. Additional purl stitches between the cables will result in a flatter, less-elastic ribbing.

Variation #2: Expanding Variation #1 over six stitches forms a vertical cable often seen in Aran designs.

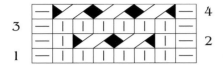

Panel of 8 stitches

Rows 1 and 3 (WS): K1, p6, k1
Row 2: P1, k1, (1/1 RC) twice, k1, p1
Row 4: P1, (1/1 RC) three times, p1

Pattern 2.3: It's easy to make the leap from repeated 1/1 right and left crossings to combinations of those crosses which form zig-zagging lines. As in the previous examples, each crossing row or round alternates with a row or round of plain knitting.

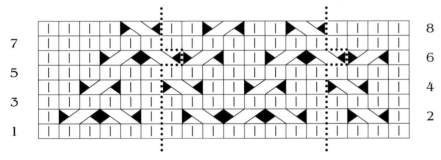

Multiple of 8 stitches + 10

Row 1 and all other WS rows: Purl
Row 2: K1, 1/1 LC, k1, *k1, 1/1 LC, 1/1 RC, 1/1 LC, k1; rep from *, end k1, 1/1 LC, 1/1 RC, k1
Row 4: K2, 1/1 LC, *k2, 1/1 RC, k2, 1/1 LC; rep from *, end k2, 1/1 RC, k2
Row 6: K1, 1/1 RC, *1/1 LC, 1/1 RC, k2, 1/1 RC; rep from *, end 1/1 LC, 1/1 RC, k3
Row 8: K4, *k1, 1/1 LC, k2, 1/1 RC, k2, rep from *, end 1/1 LC, k4

Pattern 2.4: Zig-zagging lines lead naturally to outlines of geometric shapes and trellis formations. In this example, the 1/1 knit crosses form a diamond trellis on a plain stockinette background.

Multiple of 8 stitches + 10

Row 1 and all other WS rows: Purl
Row 2: K3, 1/1 RC, *1/1 LC, k4, 1/1 RC; rep from *, end 1/1 LC, k3
Row 4: K2, 1/1 RC, k1, *k1, 1/1 LC, k2, 1/1 RC, k1; rep from *, end k1, 1/1 LC, k2
Row 6: K1, 1/1 RC, k2, *k2, 1/1 LC, 1/1 RC, k2; rep from *, end k2, 1/1 LC, k1
Row 8: K5, *k3, 1/1 RC, k3; rep from *, end k5
Row 10: K1, 1/1 LC, k2; *k2, 1/1 RC, 1/1 LC, k2; rep from *, end k2, 1/1 RC, k1
Row 12: K2, 1/1 LC, k1, *k1, 1/1 RC, k2, 1/1 LC, k1; rep from *, end k1, 1/1 RC, k2
Row 14: K3, 1/1 LC, *1/1 RC, k4, 1/1 LC; rep from *, end 1/1 RC, k3
Row 16: K4, *1/1 LC, k6; rep from *, end 1/1 LC, k4

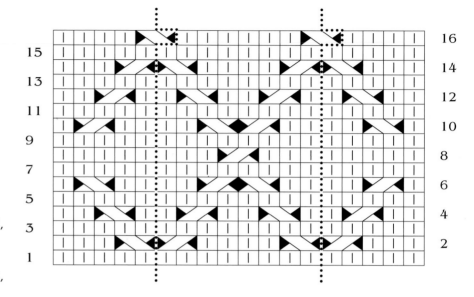

Ideas for Further Exploration

1. Make the diamonds larger or smaller by changing the number of knit stitches between the RC/LC pairs on row 2, and changing the number of rows to match.

2. Fill selected diamonds with garter or other textured stitches for additional interest, or embroider a design.

3. Repeat rows 7 and 8 and rows 15 and 16 once—this elongates the diamond pattern and adds another twist at the point where the lines meet and cross.

Pattern 2.5: In the following examples, 1/1 knit crosses have been isolated and flanked by one or more purl stitches. Setting them off in this way provides emphasis and forms cable patterns that are recognizable elements of Aran sweater design.

Stacking crossed knit stitches on top of each other forms a simple rope cable (left photo), often used as a visual divider between patterns in Aran sweaters.

Stacking the stitches, but crossing them alternately in different directions, forms a small wave cable (right photo).

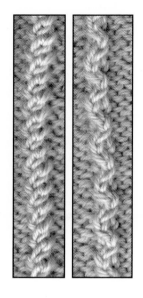

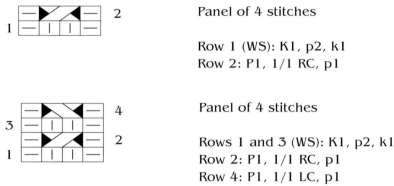

Panel of 4 stitches

Row 1 (WS): K1, p2, k1
Row 2: P1, 1/1 RC, p1

Panel of 4 stitches

Rows 1 and 3 (WS): K1, p2, k1
Row 2: P1, 1/1 RC, p1
Row 4: P1, 1/1 LC, p1

Variation #1: Each of these cables can be "doubled"—that is, two cables crossing in opposite directions can be placed immediately adjacent to each other to form new cables. When a 1/1 rope cable is doubled, it forms a small horseshoe pattern (left photo). When a 1/1 wave cable is doubled, it forms a smaller version of the familiar Aran Honeycomb cable (right photo).

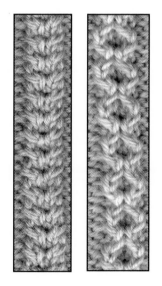

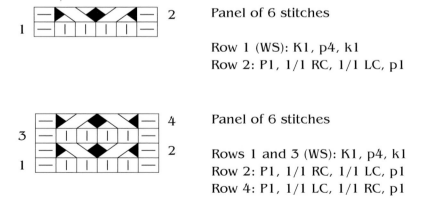

Panel of 6 stitches

Row 1 (WS): K1, p4, k1
Row 2: P1, 1/1 RC, 1/1 LC, p1

Panel of 6 stitches

Rows 1 and 3 (WS): K1, p4, k1
Row 2: P1, 1/1 RC, 1/1 LC, p1
Row 4: P1, 1/1 LC, 1/1 RC, p1

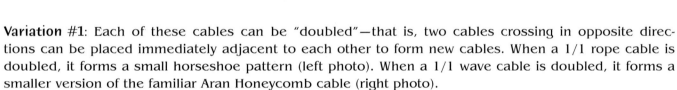

Variation #2: The miniature Aran Honeycomb cable can be worked either as a single vertical cable, or repeated over a multiple of four stitches, forming an Aran Honeycomb panel.

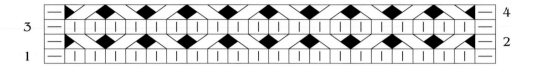

Panel of 22 stitches

Rows 1 and 3 (WS): K1, p20, k1
Row 2: P1, *1/1 RC, 1/1 LC; rep from * to last stitch, p1
Row 4: P1, *1/1 LC, 1/1 RC; rep from * to last stitch, p1

Ideas for Further Exploration

1. Add two rows of plain knitting between crossing rows in the Aran Honeycomb cable or panel to elongate the design. The centers of the elongated stitch may be filled with reverse stockinette stitch or garter stitch for additional interest.

2. Repeat the narrow vertical cables across the width of the fabric for decorative alternatives to ribbing. Note that these alternative ribbings will be less elastic than regular ribbings.

Pattern 2.6: Plait cables are formed by alternating right and left crosses over a multiple of three stitches (plaits differ from braids in that there are no purl stitches between the knit stitches—all stitches in a plait are knitted). On each crossing row of a three-stitch plait, either a 1/1 right or 1/1 left cable is worked on two of the stitches, while the remaining stitch is knitted.

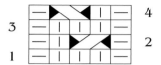

Panel of 5 stitches

Rows 1 and 3 (WS): K1, p3, k1
Row 2: P1, 1/1 RC, k1, p1
Row 4: P1, k1, 1/1 LC, p1

1/1 Purl Crosses, Cable Versions:

Crossing a knit stitch over a purl stitch makes a huge difference in the kinds of cable crossings available to knitters. Now columns of knit stitches can move across reverse stockinette stitch backgrounds, and geometric shapes can be filled with many kinds of pattern stitches.

1/1 Right Purl Cross

1. Slip the next stitch to a cable needle and hold at the back of the work.

2. Knit the next stitch from the left-hand needle.

3. Purl the stitch from the cable needle.

1/1 Left Purl Cross

1. Slip the next stitch to a cable needle and hold at the front of the work.

2. Purl the next stitch from the left-hand needle.

3. Knit the stitch from the cable needle.

1/1 Purl Crosses, Twist Versions: These are much easier and faster to work than the cable versions.

1. Bring the right-hand needle in front of the first stitch and knit into the second stitch.

2. Purl the skipped stitch, dropping both from the needle together.

1/1 Right Purl Cross

1. Bring the right-hand needle behind the first stitch and purl into the back of the second stitch.

2. Knit into the front of the skipped stitch, dropping both from the needle together.

1/1 Left Purl Cross

Pattern 2.7: Combining 1/1 right and left purl crosses allows for the movement of single columns of knit stitches back and forth over a reverse stockinette background. These lines can be tight and angular, or loose and undulating, depending upon the number of intervening non-cabling rows between cabling rows. In this example, a single column of knit stitches moves alternately to the left and right by two stitches.

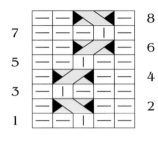

Panel of 5 stitches

Rows 1 and 5 (WS): K2, p1, k2
Row 2: P2, 1/1 LPC, p1
Row 3: K1, p1, k3
Row 4: P2, 1/1 RPC, p1
Row 6: P1, 1/1 RPC, p2
Row 7: K3, p1, k1
Row 8: P1, 1/1 LPC, p2

Variation: Knit stitches can travel in pairs, or even in groups of three stitches or more. Here, the two knit stitches are separated by two purl stitches, and the lines move to the left by five stitches, then to the right.

Panel of 11 stitches

Row 1 (WS): K1, p1, k2, p1, k6
Row 2: P5, 1/1 RPC, p1, 1/1 RPC, p1
Row 3: K2, p1, k2, p1, k5
Row 4: P4, 1/1 RPC, p1, 1/1 RPC, p2
Row 5: K3, p1, k2, p1, k4
Row 6: P3, 1/1 RPC, p1, 1/1 RPC, p3
Row 7: K4, p1, k2, p1, k3
Row 8: P2, 1/1 RPC, p1, 1/1 RPC, p4
Row 9: K5, p1, k2, p1, k2
Row 10: P1, 1/1 RPC, p1, 1/1 RPC, p5

Row 11: K6, p1, k2, p1, k1
Row 12: P1, 1/1 LPC, p1, 1/1 LPC, p5
Row 13: K5, p1, k2, p1, k2
Row 14: P2, 1/1 LPC, p1, 1/1 LPC, p4
Row 15: K4, p1, k2, p1, k3
Row 16: P3, 1/1 LPC, p1, 1/1 LPC, p3
Row 17: K3, p1, k2, p1, k4
Row 18: P4, 1/1 LPC, p1, 1/1 LPC, p2
Row 19: K2, p1, k2, p1, k5
Row 20: P5, 1/1 LPC, p1, 1/1 LPC, p1

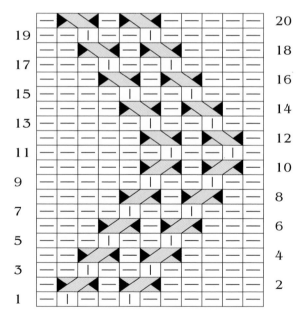

Pattern 2.8: Zig-zagging columns of knit stitches form allover hourglass patterns. The knit stitches move over the fabric and meet—but do not cross.

Multiple of 8 stitches + 2

Row 1 (WS): K1, *p1, k6, p1; rep from *, end k1
Row 2: P1, *1/1 LPC, p4, 1/1 RPC; rep from *, end p1
Row 3: K1, *k1, p1, k4, p1, k1; rep from *, end k1
Row 4: P1, *p1, 1/1 LPC, p2, 1/1 RPC, p1; rep from *, end p1
Row 5: K1, *k2, p1, k2, p1, k2; rep from *, end k1
Row 6: P1, *p2, 1/1 LPC, 1/1 RPC, p2; rep from *, end p1
Row 7: K1, *k3, p2, k3; rep from *, end k1
Row 8: P1, *p2, 1/1 RPC, 1/1 LPC, p2; rep from *, end p1
Row 9: K1, *k2, p1, k2, p1, k2; rep from *, end k1
Row 10: P1, *p1, 1/1 RPC, p2, 1/1 LPC, p1; rep from *, end p1
Row 11: K1, *k1, p1, k4, p1, k1; rep from *, end k1
Row 12: P1, *1/1 RPC, p4, 1/1 LPC; rep from *, end p1

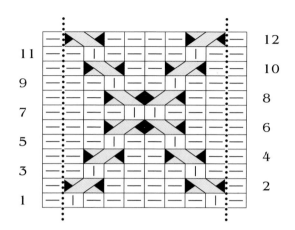

Variation: Double the lines, moving them in parallel, for a more intricate version of the hourglass shape.

Multiple of 14 stitches + 2

Row 1 (WS): K1, *p1, k2, p1, k6, p1, k2, p1; rep from *, end k1

Row 2: P1, *1/1 LPC, p1, 1/1 LPC, p4, 1/1 RPC, p1, 1/1 RPC; rep from *, end p1

Row 3: K1, *k1, p1, k2, p1, k4, p1, k2, p1, k1; rep from *, end k1

Row 4: P1, *(p1, 1/1 LPC) twice, p2, (1/1 RPC, p1) twice; rep from *, end p1

Row 5: K1, *(k2, p1) twice, k2, (p1, k2) twice; rep from *, end k1

Row 6: P1, *p2, 1/1 LPC, p1, 1/1 LPC, 1/1 RPC, p1, 1/1 RPC, p2; rep from *, end p1

Row 7: K1, *k3, p1, k2, p2, k2, p1, k3; rep from *, end k1

Row 8: P1, *p2, 1/1 RPC, p1, 1/1 RPC, 1/1 LPC, p1, 1/1 LPC, p2; rep from *, end p1

Row 9: K1, *(k2, p1) twice, k2, (p1, k2) twice; rep from *, end k1

Row 10: P1, *(p1, 1/1 RPC) twice, p2, (1/1 LPC, p1) twice; rep from *, end p1

Row 11: K1, *k1, p1, k2, p1, k4, p1, k2, p1, k1; rep from *, end k1

Row 12: P1, *1/1 RPC, p1, 1/1 RPC, p4, 1/1 LPC, p1, 1/1 LPC; rep from *, end p1

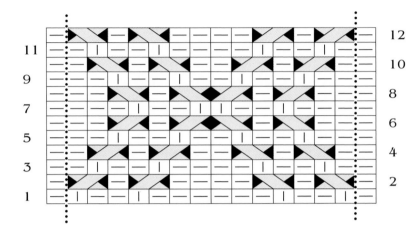

Pattern 2.9: Just as with the 1/1 knit crosses, zig-zagging lines incorporating 1/1 purl crosses lead naturally to trellis patterns. The simplest of trellis patterns is formed when 1/1 right and left crosses move back and forth by one stitch over a purl background, meeting and crossing over each other as 1/1 knit crosses. This simple pattern lends itself to many expanded variations.

Multiple of 4 stitches + 6

Row 1 (WS): K2, *p2, k2; rep from * to end
Row 2: *P2, 1/1 RC; rep from *, end p2
Row 3: K2, *p2, k2; rep from * to end
Row 4: P1, 1/1 RPC, *1/1 LPC, 1/1 RPC; rep from *, end 1/1 LPC, p1
Row 5: K1, p1, k1, *k1, p2, k1; rep from *, end k1, p1, k1
Row 6: P1, k1, p1, *p1, 1/1 LC, p1; rep from *, end p1, k1, p1
Row 7: K1, p1, k1, *k1, p2, k1; rep from *, end k1, p1, k1
Row 8: P1, 1/1 LPC, *1/1 RPC, 1/1 LPC; rep from *, end 1/1 RPC, p1

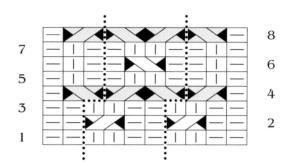

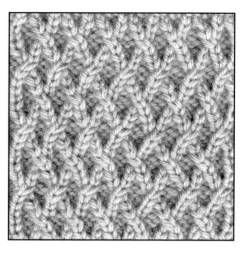

Variation #1: Increase the number of background stitches the knit columns must traverse before they meet and cross over each other. In this example, the knit stitches cross over three purl stitches, then meet and cross over each other.

Multiple of 8 stitches + 10

Row 1 (WS): K4, *p2, k6; rep from *, end p2, k4
Row 2: P4, 1/1 LC, *p6, 1/1 LC; rep from *, end p4
Row 3: K4, *p2, k6; rep from *, end p2, k4
Row 4: P3, 1/1 RPC, *1/1 LPC, p4, 1/1 RPC; rep from *, end 1/1 LPC, p3
Row 5: K3, p1, k1, *k1, p1, k4, p1, k1; rep from *, end k1, p1, k3
Row 6: P2, 1/1 RPC, p1, *p1, 1/1 LPC, p2, 1/1 RPC, p1; rep from *, end p1, 1/1 LPC, p2
Row 7: K2, p1, k2, *(k2, p1) twice, k2; rep from *, end k2, p1, k2
Row 8: P1, 1/1 RPC, p2, *p2, 1/1 LPC, 1/1 RPC, p2; rep from *, end p2, 1/1 LPC, p1
Row 9: K1, p1, k3, *k3, p2, k3; rep from *, end k3, p1, k1
Row 10: P1, k1, p3, *p3, 1/1 RC, p3; rep from *, end p3, k1, p1
Row 11: K1, p1, k3, *k3, p2, k3; rep from *, end k3, p1, k1
Row 12: P1, 1/1 LPC, p2, *p2, 1/1 RPC, 1/1 LPC, p2; rep from *, end p2, 1/1 RPC, p1
Row 13: K2, p1, k2, *(k2, p1) twice, k2; rep from *, end k2, p1, k2

Row 14: P2, 1/1 LPC, p1, *p1, 1/1
 RPC, p2, 1/1 LPC, p1; rep
 from *, end p1, 1/1 RPC, p2
Row 15: K3, p1, k1, *k1, p1, k4,
 p1, k1; rep from *, end k1,
 p1, k3
Row 16: P3, 1/1 LPC, *1/1 RPC,
 p4, 1/1 LPC; rep from *, end
 1/1 RPC, p3

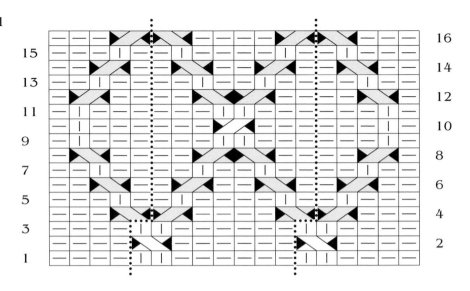

Variation #2: Increase the number of times the knit stitches cross over each other. In this example, rows 1 and 2 of the chart in the previous example are worked twice, as are rows 9 and 10. This elongates the diamonds and makes the trellis pattern more intricate.

Multiple of 8 stitches + 10

Row 1 (WS): K4, *p2, k6; rep from *, end p2, k4
Row 2: P4, 1/1 LC, *p6, 1/1 LC; rep from *, end p4
Row 3: K4, *p2, k6; rep from *, end p2, k4
Row 4: P4, 1/1 LC, *p6, 1/1 LC; rep from *, end p4
Row 5: K4, *p2, k6; rep from *, end p2, k4
Row 6: P3, 1/1 RPC, *1/1 LPC, p4, 1/1 RPC; rep from *, end 1/1 LPC, p3
Row 7: K3, p1, k1, *k1, p1, k4, p1, k1; rep from *, end k1, p1, k3
Row 8: P2, 1/1 RPC, p1, *p1, 1/1 LPC, p2, 1/1 RPC, p1; rep from *, end p1, 1/1 LPC, p2
Row 9: K2, p1, k2, *(k2, p1) twice, k2; rep from *, end k2, p1, k2
Row 10: P1, 1/1 RPC, p2, *p2, 1/1 LPC, 1/1 RPC, p2; rep from *, end p2, 1/1 LPC, p1
Row 11: K1, p1, k3, *k3, p2, k3; rep from *, end k3, p1, k1
Row 12: P1, k1, p3, *p3, 1/1 RC, p3; rep from *, end p3, k1, p1
Row 13: K1, p1, k3, *k3, p2, k3; rep from *, end k3, p1, k1
Row 14: P1, k1, p3, *p3, 1/1 RC, p3; rep from *, end p3, k1, p1
Row 15: K1, p1, k3, *k3, p2, k3; rep from *, end k3, p1, k1

Row 16: P1, 1/1 LPC, p2, *p2, 1/1 RPC, 1/1 LPC, p2; rep from *, end p2, 1/1 RPC, p1

Row 17: K2, p1, k2, *(k2, p1) twice, k2; rep from *, end k2, p1, k2

Row 18: P2, 1/1 LPC, p1, *p1, 1/1 RPC, p2, 1/1 LPC, p1; rep from *, end p1, 1/1 RPC, p2

Row 19: K3, p1, k1, *k1, p1, k4, p1, k1; rep from *, end k1, p1, k3

Row 20: P3, 1/1 LPC, *1/1 RPC, p4, 1/1 LPC; rep from *, end 1/1 RPC, p3

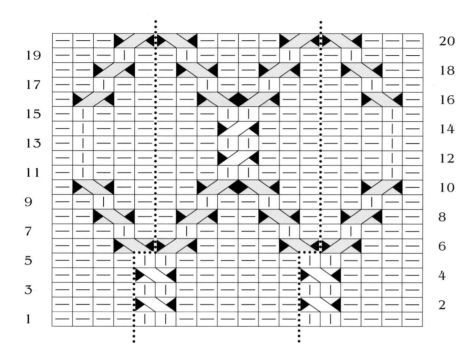

Ideas for Further Exploration

1. Fill the diamonds of the trellis with moss stitch, garter stitch, or some other filler stitch.

2. Embroider or embellish the centers of plain diamonds.

Pattern 2.10: Isolate one multiple of a trellis pattern to form a panel of diamonds.

Panel of 12 stitches

Row 1 (WS): K5, p2, k5
Row 2: P5, 1/1 RC, p5
Row 3: K5, p2, k5
Row 4: P4, 1/1 RPC, 1/1 LPC, p4
Row 5: K4, p1, k2, p1, k4
Row 6: P3, 1/1 RPC, p2, 1/1 LPC, p3
Row 7: K3, p1, k4, p1, k3
Row 8: P2, 1/1 RPC, p4, 1/1 LPC, p2
Row 9: K2, p1, k6, p1, k2
Row 10: P1, 1/1 RPC, p6, 1/1 LPC, p1
Row 11: K1, p1, k8, p1, k1
Row 12: P1, 1/1 LPC, p6, 1/1 RPC, p1
Row 13: K2, p1, k6, p1, k2
Row 14: P2, 1/1 LPC, p4, 1/1 RPC, p2
Row 15: K3, p1, k4, p1, k3
Row 16: P3, 1/1 LPC, p2, 1/1 RPC, p3
Row 17: K4, p1, k2, p1, k4
Row 18: P4, 1/1 LPC, 1/1 RPC, p4

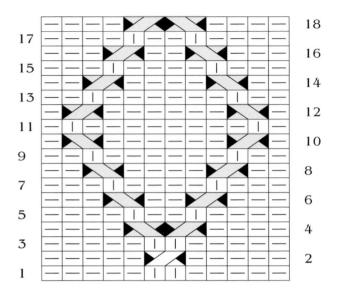

Variation #1: Remove two of the cabling rows and add non-cabling rows at the outside points of the diamond to create a rounder shape.

Panel of 10 stitches

Row 1 (WS): K4, p2, k4
Row 2: P4, 1/1 RC, p4
Row 3: K4, p2, k4
Row 4: P3, 1/1 RPC, 1/1 LPC, p3
Row 5: K3, p1, k2, p1, k3
Row 6: P2, 1/1 RPC, p2, 1/1 LPC, p2
Row 7: K2, p1, k4, p1, k2
Row 8: P1, 1/1 RPC, p4, 1/1 LPC, p1
Row 9: K1, p1, k6, p1, k1
Row 10: P1, k1, p6, k1, p1
Row 11: K1, p1, k6, p1, k1
Row 12: P1, 1/1 LPC, p4, 1/1 RPC, p1
Row 13: K2, p1, k4, p1, k2
Row 14: P2, 1/1 LPC, p2, 1/1 RPC, p2
Row 15: K3, p1, k2, p1, k3
Row 16: P3, 1/1 LPC, 1/1 RPC, p3

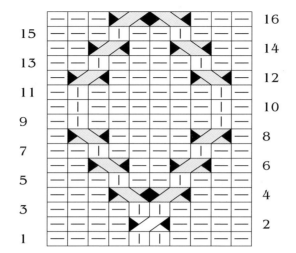

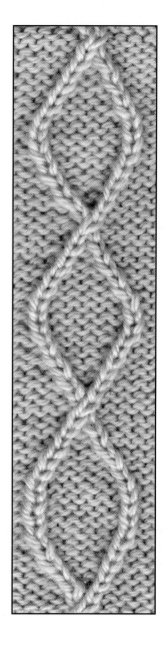

Variation #2: Elongate the cable by adding crossing rows; in this example, rows 1 and 2 of the original pattern are worked twice.

Panel of 12 stitches

Row 1 (WS): K5, p2, k5
Row 2: P5, 1/1 RC, p5
Row 3: K5, p2, k5
Row 4: P5, 1/1 RC, p5
Row 5: K5, p2, k5
Row 6: P4, 1/1 RPC, 1/1 LPC, p4
Row 7: K4, p1, k2, p1, k4
Row 8: P3, 1/1 RPC, p2, 1/1 LPC, p3
Row 9: K3, p1, k4, p1, k3
Row 10: P2, 1/1 RPC, p4, 1/1 LPC, p2
Row 11: K2, p1, k6, p1, k2
Row 12: P1, 1/1 RPC, p6, 1/1 LPC, p1
Row 13: K1, p1, k8, p1, k1
Row 14: P1, 1/1 LPC, p6, 1/1 RPC, p1
Row 15: K2, p1, k6, p1, k2
Row 16: P2, 1/1 LPC, p4, 1/1 RPC, p2
Row 17: K3, p1, k4, p1, k3
Row 18: P3, 1/1 LPC, p2, 1/1 RPC, p3
Row 19: K4, p1, k2, p1, k4
Row 20: P4, 1/1 LPC, 1/1 RPC, p4

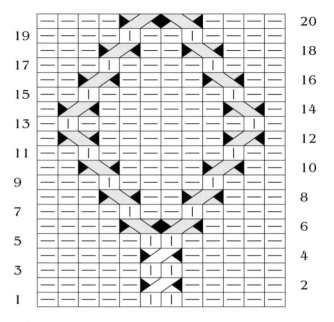

Ideas for Further Exploration

1. Fill the diamonds of the trellis with moss stitch, garter stitch, or some other filler stitch.

2. Embroider or embellish the centers of plain diamonds.

3. Place diamonds in half-drop formation, but add a single zig-zagging knit line separating them.

Variation #3: Place the diamonds in half-drop formation—the diamonds are adjacent to each other, but one of them is "dropped" half the number of rows of the repeat and nested between the others. A panel of 28 stitches is shown here, but this can also be used as an allover pattern.

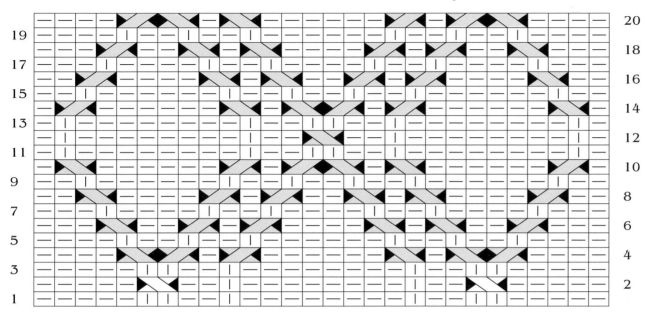

Panel of 28 stitches

Rows 1 and 3 (WS): K5, p2, k2, p1, k8, p1, k2, p2, k5

Row 2: P5, 1/1 LC, p2, k1, p8, k1, p2, 1/1 LC, p5

Row 4: P4, 1/1 RPC, 1/1 LPC, p1, 1/1 LPC, p6, 1/1 RPC, p1, 1/1 RPC, 1/1 LPC, p4

Rows 5 and 19: K4, p1, (k2, p1) twice, k6, (p1, k2) twice, p1, k4

Row 6: P3, 1/1 RPC, p2, 1/1 LPC, p1, 1/1 LPC, p4, 1/1 RPC, p1, 1/1 RPC, p2, 1/1 LPC, p3

Rows 7 and 17: K3, p1, k4, p1, k2, p1, k4, p1, k2, p1, k4, p1, k3

Row 8: P2, 1/1 RPC, p4, 1/1 LPC, p1, 1/1 LPC, p2, 1/1 RPC, p1, 1/1 RPC, p4, 1/1 LPC, p2

Rows 9 and 15: K2, p1, k6, p1, (k2, p1) three times, k6, p1, k2

Row 10: P1, 1/1 RPC, p6, 1/1 LPC, p1, 1/1 LPC, 1/1 RPC, p1, 1/1 RPC, p6, 1/1 LPC, p1

Rows 11 and 13: K1, p1, k8, p1, k2, p2, k2, p1, k8, p1, k1

Row 12: P1, k1, p8, k1, p2, 1/1 LC, p2, k1, p8, k1, p1

Row 14: P1, 1/1 LPC, p6, 1/1 RPC, p1, 1/1 RPC, 1/1 LPC, p1, 1/1 LPC, p6, 1/1 RPC, p1

Row 16: P2, 1/1 LPC, p4, 1/1 RPC, p1, 1/1 RPC, p2, 1/1 LPC, p1, 1/1 LPC, p4, 1/1 RPC, p2

Row 18: P3, 1/1 LPC, p2, 1/1 RPC, p1, 1/1 RPC, p4, 1/1 LPC, p1, 1/1 LPC, p2, 1/1 RPC, p3

Row 20: P4, 1/1 LPC, 1/1 RPC, p1, 1/1 RPC, p6, 1/1 LPC, p1, 1/1 LPC, 1/1 RPC, p4

1/1 All-Purl Crosses, Twist Versions: To this point, we've discussed patterns in which crosses happen only on right-side rows. Interesting effects can be achieved when crosses happen on both right- and wrong-side rows. The instructions on these two pages illustrate how to twist stitches on wrong-side rows.

1/1 Right All-Purl Cross, Twist Version 1

1. Bring the right-hand needle in front of the first stitch and purl the second stitch.

2. Purl the skipped stitch, and drop both stitches from the left-hand needle together.

1/1 Right All-Purl Cross, Twist Version 2

1. Bring the right-hand needle in front of the first stitch and purl the second stitch.

2. Purl together the skipped stitch and the second stitch, then drop both stitches from the left-hand needle together.

1. Slip two stitches one at a time as if to knit, then return them to the left-hand needle in the turned position.

2. Purl them together through the backs of the loops, then purl the first stitch again through the back of its loop. Drop both stitches from the left-hand needle together.

1/1 Left All-Purl Cross, Twist Version

1/1 Crosses on Every Row:

Bavarian stitch patterns could be considered a subset of this group of cable patterns, as they also feature crosses on both right- and wrong-side rows. However, in Bavarian stitch patterns, each stitch is also twisted (that is, worked through its back loop) as it is knitted/purled or crossed. The patterns included in this section do not require the stitches to be twisted.

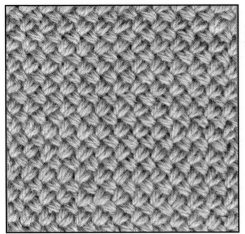

Pattern 2.11: Working adjacent 1/1 knit crosses on both right- and wrong-side rows forms a tight basketweave pattern. This pattern benefits from being worked on slightly larger needles than would normally be used.

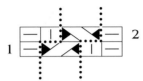

Multiple of 2 stitches + 3

Row 1 (WS): K1, *1/1 RC; rep from *, end p1, k1
Row 2: P1, *1/1 LC; rep from *, end k1, p1

Pattern 2.12 A useful narrow cable pattern results from working 1/1 knit crosses on both the public- and private-rows of a two-stitch knit rib. This cable can be used as a single divider between larger cable patterns, or repeated across the width of a fabric for a decorative ribbing pattern.

Panel of 4 stitches

Row 1 (WS): K1, 1/1 RC, k1
Row 2: P1, 1/1 LC, p1

Pattern 2.13: Working 1/1 crosses on both right- and wrong-side rows of a three-stitch knit rib results in a tight plait pattern.

Panel of 5 stitches

Row 1 (WS): K1, 1/1 RC, p1, k1
Row 2: P1, 1/1 LC, k1, p1

Three-Stitch Crosses

Three-stitch crosses are an interesting group. Some members of this group make only occasional appearances, but their presence really spices up the show. Others are the anchor behind many popular cable patterns, which wouldn't be possible without them.

Adding a third stitch to the group of stitches participating in the cross opens up a whole new world of possibilities: one stitch crossing over two, two stitches crossing over one, and two outside stitches exchanging places over a central stitch. As you look through this chapter, note the interesting textural effects that are possible when three stitches exchange places within the knitted fabric.

1/2 Knit Crosses:
In these crosses, one knit stitch crosses to the right or left over two knit stitches. Some instructions specify that the crossing stitch be slipped purlwise one or two rows prior to the cross, but I find this unnecessary except when working two-color slip-stitch cable patterns. It stretches out the crossing stitch and draws up the fabric, something which may or may not be desirable.

1/2 Right Cross

1. Slip the next two stitches to a cable needle and hold at the back of the work.

2. Knit the next stitch from the left-hand needle.

3. Knit the two stitches from the cable needle.

1/2 Left Cross

1. Slip the next stitch to a cable needle and hold at the front of the work.

2. Knit the next two stitches from the left-hand needle.

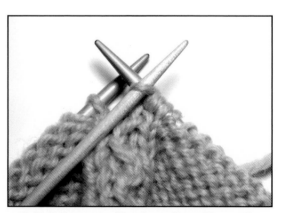

3. Knit the next stitch from the cable needle.

Pattern 3.1: In this pattern, 1/2 right and left crosses are used as accents on a stockinette stitch background. This is a wonderful allover pattern and a great alternative to plain stockinette stitch.

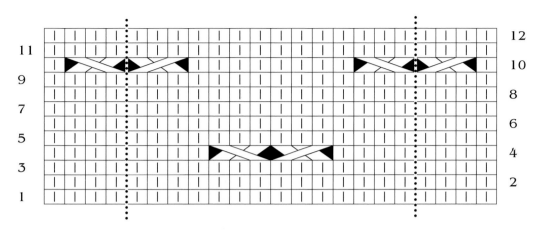

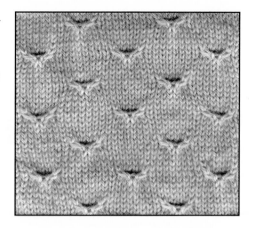

Multiple of 14 stitches + 8

Row 1 and all other WS rows: Purl

Rows 2, 6, 8 and 12: Knit

Row 4: K4, *k4, 1/2 RC, 1/2 LC, k4; rep from *, end k4

Row 10: K1, 1/2 RC, *1/2 LC, k8, 1/2 RC; rep from *, end 1/2 LC, k1

Pattern 3.2: Doubling the 1/2 knit crosses in opposite directions forms a horseshoe-style cable.

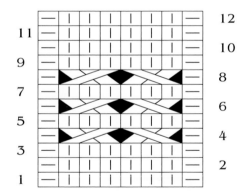

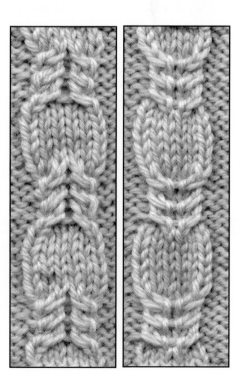

Panel of 8 stitches

Row 1 and all other WS rows: K1, p6, k1
Rows 2, 10 and 12: P1, k6, p1
Rows 4, 6 and 8: P1, 1/2 LC, 1/2 RC, p1

Panel of 8 stitches

Row 1 and all other WS rows: K1, p6, k1
Rows 2, 10 and 12: P1, k6, p1
Rows 4, 6 and 8: P1, 1/2 RC, 1/2 LC, p1

1/2 Purl Crosses: Need to simulate a branch or a vine snaking across the fabric? These cables—in which one knit stitch crosses over two purl stitches—are the ones for the job. They appear in many "floral"–themed cable patterns.

1/2 Right Purl Cross

1. Slip the next two stitches to a cable needle and hold at the back of the work.

2. Knit the next stitch from the left-hand needle.

3. Purl the two stitches from the cable needle.

1/2 Left Purl Cross

1. Slip the next stitch to a cable needle and hold at the front of the work.

2. Purl the next two stitches from the left-hand needle.

3. Knit the stitch from the left-hand needle.

Pattern 3.3: This is a wonderful cable pattern featuring 1/2 right and left purl crosses. It "flips" horizontally halfway through the row repeat, so that rows 13-24 are a mirror-image of rows 1-12.

Panel of 16 stitches

Row 1 (WS): K6, p3, k7

Row 2: P4, MK, p2, 1/2 RPC, p6

Row 3: K8, p1, k2, p1, k4

Row 4: P1, MK, p2, 1/1 LPC, p1, k1tbl, p3, MK, p4

Row 5: K4, p1, k3, p1, k1, p1, k3, p1, k1

Row 6: P1, 1/2 LPC, p1, 1/1 LPC, k1tbl, p1, 1/2 RPC, p2, MK, p1

Row 7: K1, p1, k4, p1, k1, p2, k2, p1, k3

Row 8: P3, 1/2 LPC, 1/1 LPC, 1/1 RPC, p2, 1/2 RPC, p1

Row 9: K3, p1, k3, p2, k1, p1, k5

Row 10: P5, 1/1 LPC, 1/1 RPC, p1, 1/2 RPC, p3

Row 11: K5, p1, k2, p2, k6

Row 12: P6, 1/1 LC, 1/2 RPC, p5

Row 13: K7, p3, k6

Row 14: P6, 1/2 LPC, p2, MK, p4

Row 15: K4, p1, k2, p1, k8

Row 16: P4, MK, p3, k1tbl, p1, 1/1 RPC, p2, MK, p1

Row 17: K1, p1, k3, p1, k1, p1, k3, p1, k4

Row 18: P1, MK, p2, 1/2 LPC, p1, k1tbl, 1/1 RPC, p1, 1/2 RPC, p1

Row 19: K3, p1, k2, p2, k1, p1, k4, p1, k1

Row 20: P1, 1/2 LPC, p2, 1/1 LPC, 1/1 RPC, 1/2 RPC, p3

Row 21: K5, p1, k1, p2, k3, p1, k3

Row 22: P3, 1/2 LPC, p1, 1/1 LPC, 1/1 RPC, p5

Row 23: K6, p2, k2, p1, k5

Row 24: P5, 1/2 LPC, 1/1 RC, p6

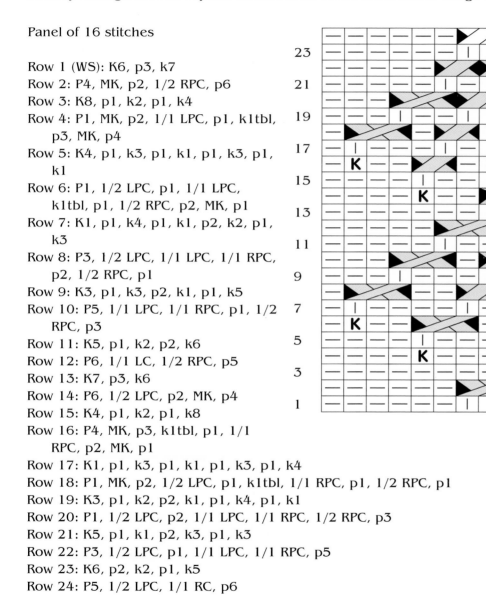

2/1 Knit Crosses: These are such a subtle cables that I really had to search my stitch dictionaries to find examples of their use.

2/1 Right Cross

1. Slip the next stitch to a cable needle and hold at the back of the work.

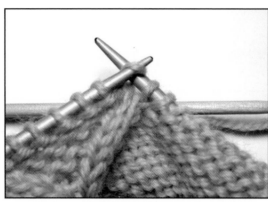

2. Knit the next two stitches from the left-hand needle.

3. Knit the stitch from the cable needle.

2/1 Left Cross

1. Slip the next two stitches to a cable needle and hold at the front of the work.

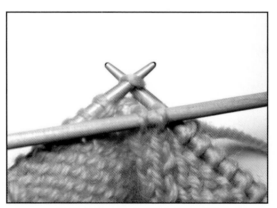

2. Knit the next stitch from the left-hand needle.

3. Knit the two stitches from the cable needle.

Pattern 3.4: Here, the two-stitch knit ribs travel across a stockinette background, forming a branching pattern.

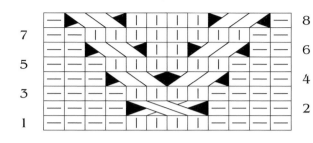

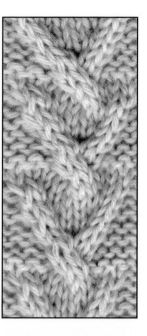

Panel of 12 stitches

Row 1 (WS): K4, p4, k4
Row 2: P4, 2/2 LC, p4
Row 3: K4, p4, k4
Row 4: P3, 2/1 RC, 2/1 LC, p3
Row 5: K3, p6, k3
Row 6: P2, 2/1 RC, k2, 2/1 LC, p2
Row 7: K2, p8, k2
Row 8: P1, 2/1 RC, k4, 2/1 LC, p1

Variation: Mirror-image the "V" vertically to create a diamond shape and fill the center with garter stitch. Note that the two-stitch knit ribs meet, but do not cross.

Panel of 14 stitches

Row 1 (WS): K1, p12, k1
Row 2: P1, k3, 2/1 RC, 2/1 LC, k3, p1
Rows 3 and 15: K1, p5, k2, p5, k1
Row 4: P1, k2, 2/1 RC, k2, 2/1 LC, k2, p1
Rows 5 and 13: K1, p4, k4, p4, k1
Row 6: P1, k1, 2/1 RC, k4, 2/1 LC, k1, p1
Rows 7 and 11: K1, p3, k6, p3, k1
Row 8: P1, 2/1 RC, k6, 2/1 LC, p1
Row 9: K1, p2, k8, p2, k1
Row 10: P1, 2/1 LC, k6, 2/1 RC, p1
Row 12: P1, k1, 2/1 LC, k4, 2/1 RC, k1, p1
Row 14: P1, k2, 2/1 LC, k2, 2/1 RC, k2, p1
Row 16: P1, k3, 2/1 LC, 2/1 RC, k3, p1

2/1 Purl Crosses: These crosses are the stars of the three-stitch cable show. They feature so often in cable patterns that I sometimes wonder how we would be able to cable without them.

2/1 Right Purl Cross

1. Slip the next stitch to a cable needle and hold at the back of the work.

2. Knit the next two stitches from the left-hand needle.

3. Purl the stitch from the cable needle.

2/1 Left Purl Cross

1. Slip the next two stitches to a cable needle and hold at the front of the work.

2. Purl the next stitch from the left-hand needle.

3. Knit the two stitches from the cable needle.

Pattern 3.5: This pattern is similar to Pattern 3.4, except that the 2/1 right and left *knit* crosses have been replaced by 2/1 right and left *purl* crosses.

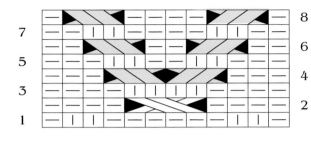

Panel of 12 stitches

Row 1 (WS): K1, p2, k6, p2, k1
Row 2: P4, 2/2 LC, p4
Row 3: K4, p4, k4
Row 4: P3, 2/1 RPC, 2/1 LPC, p3
Row 5: K3, p2, k2, p2, k3
Row 6: P2, 2/1 RPC, p2, 2/1 LPC, p2
Row 7: K2, p2, k4, p2, k2
Row 8: P1, 2/1 RPC, p4, 2/1 LPC, p1

Pattern 3.6: This is a zig-zag pattern incorporating 2/1 right and left purl crosses. A two-stitch knit rib crosses to the left and then to the right over four purl stitches.

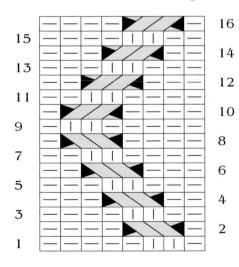

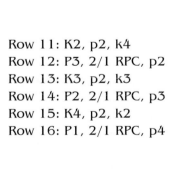

Panel of 8 stitches

Row 1 (WS): K5, p2, k1
Row 2: P1, 2/1 LPC, p4
Row 3: K4, p2, k2
Row 4: P2, 2/1 LPC, p3
Row 5: K3, p2, k3
Row 6: P3, 2/1 LPC, p2
Row 7: K2, p2, k4
Row 8: P4, 2/1 LPC, p1
Row 9: K1, p2, k5
Row 10: P4, 2/1 RPC, p1

Row 11: K2, p2, k4
Row 12: P3, 2/1 RPC, p2
Row 13: K3, p2, k3
Row 14: P2, 2/1 RPC, p3
Row 15: K4, p2, k2
Row 16: P1, 2/1 RPC, p4

Variation: Here, two pairs of two-stitch knit ribs move in opposing directions, with one pair superimposed on the other pair. Changing the 2/2 right crosses to left crosses in rows 20, 24, and 28 causes the pairs of ribs to wrap around each other instead of one rib being superimposed upon the other.

Panel of 18 stitches

Rows 1, 15, 17 and 31 (WS): K1, p2, k3, p2, k2, p2, k3, p2, k1

Row 2: P1, 2/1 LPC, p2, 2/1 LPC, 2/1 RPC, p2, 2/1 LPC, p1

Rows 3, 13, 19 and 29: K2, p2, k3, p4, k3, p2, k2

Row 4: P2, 2/1 LPC, p2, 2/2 LC, p2, 2/1 RPC, p2

Rows 5, 11, 21 and 27: K3, p2, k2, p4, k2, p2, k3

Row 6: P3, (2/1 LPC, 2/1 RPC) twice, p3

Rows 7, 9, 23 and 25: K4, p4, k2, p4, k4

Row 8: P4, 2/2 LC, p2, 2/2 LC, p4

Row 10: P3, (2/1 RPC, 2/1 LPC) twice, p3

Row 12: P2, 2/1 RPC, p2, 2/2 LC, p2, 2/1 LPC, p2

Row 14: P1, 2/1 RPC, p2, 2/1 RPC, 2/1 LPC, p2, 2/1 LPC, p1

Row 16: P1, k2, p3, k2, p2, k2, p3, k2, p1

Row 18: P1, 2/1 LPC, p2, 2/1 LPC, 2/1 RPC, p2, 2/1 RPC, p1

Row 20: P2, 2/1 LPC, p2, 2/2 RC, p2, 2/1 RPC, p2

Row 22: P3, (2/1 LPC, 2/1 RPC) twice, p3

Row 24: P4, 2/2 RC, p2, 2/2 RC, p4

Row 26: P3, (2/1 RPC, 2/1 LPC) twice, p3

Row 28: P2, 2/1 RPC, p2, 2/2 RC, p2, 2/1 LPC, p2

Row 30: P1, 2/1 RPC, p2, 2/1 RPC, 2/1 LPC, p2, 2/1 LPC, p1

Row 32: P1, k2, p3, k2, p2, k2, p3, k2, p1

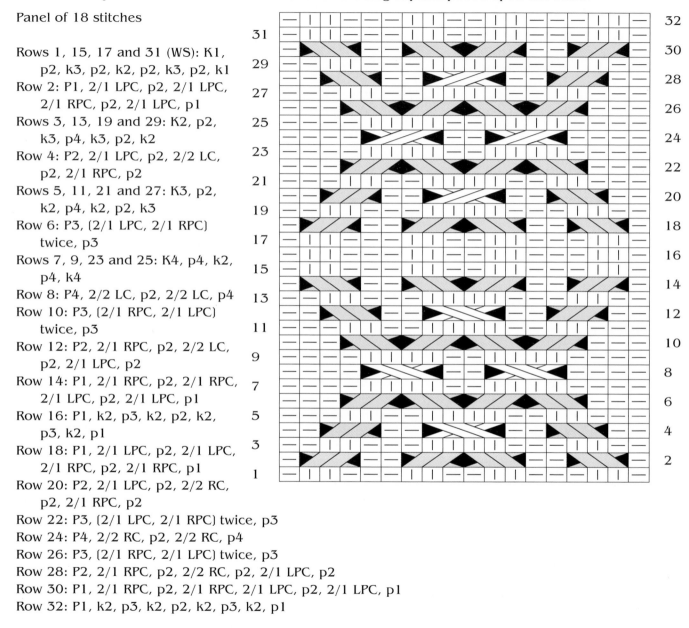

Pattern 3.7: Placing zig-zagging lines next to each other such that they meet but do not cross creates an hourglass pattern.

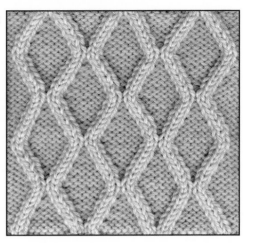

Multiple of 12 stitches + 2

Row 1 (WS): K1, *k4, p4, k4; rep from *, end k1

Row 2: P1, *p3, 2/1 RPC, 2/1 LPC, p3; rep from *, end p1

Row 3: K1, *k3, p2, k2, p2, k3; rep from *, end k1

Row 4: P1, *p2, 2/1 RPC, p2, 2/1 LPC, p2; rep from *, end p1

Row 5: K1, *k2, p2, k4, p2, k2; rep from *, end k1

Row 6: P1, *p1, 2/1 RPC, p4, 2/1 LPC, p1; rep from *, end p1

Row 7: K1, *k1, p2, k6, p2, k1; rep from *, end k1

Row 8: P1, *2/1 RPC, p6, 2/1 LPC; rep from *, end p1

Row 9: K1, *p2, k8, p2; rep from *, end k1

Row 10: P1, *2/1 LPC, p6, 2/1 RPC; rep from *, end p1

Row 11: K1, *k1, p2, k6, p2, k1; rep from *, end k1

Row 12: P1, *p1, 2/1 LPC, p4, 2/1 RPC, p1; rep from *, end p1

Row 13: K1, *k2, p2, k4, p2, k2; rep from *, end k1

Row 14: P1, *p2, 2/1 LPC, p2, 2/1 RPC, p2; rep from *, end p1

Row 15: K1, *k3, p2, k2, p2, k3; rep from *, end k1

Row 16: P1, *p3, 2/1 LPC, 2/1 RPC, p3; rep from *, end p1

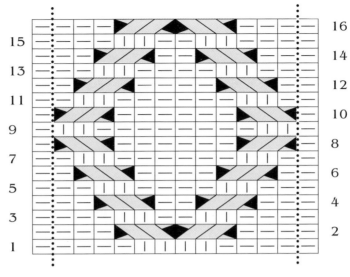

Pattern 3.8: Expanding pattern 3.7 such that the cables meet and cross results in a trellis pattern.

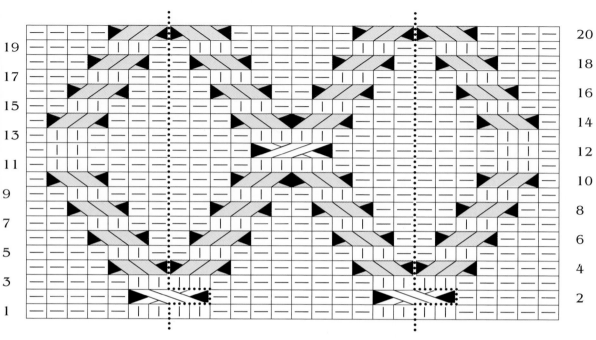

Multiple of 12 stitches +14

Rows 1 and 3 (WS): K5, p2, *p2, k8, p2; rep from *, end p2, k5

Row 2: P5, *2/2 LC, p8; rep from *, end 2/2 LC, p5

Row 4: P4, 2/1 RPC, *2/1 LPC, p6, 2/1 RPC; rep from *, end 2/1 LPC, p4

Rows 5 and 19: K4, p2, k1, *k1, p2, k6, p2, k1; rep from *, end k1, p2, k4

Row 6: P3, 2/1 RPC, p1, *p1, 2/1 LPC, p4, 2/1 RPC, p1; rep from *, end p1, 2/1 LPC, p3

Rows 7 and 17: K3, p2, k2, *k2, p2, k4, p2, k2; rep from *, end k2, p2, k3

Row 8: P2, 2/1 RPC, p2, *p2, 2/1 LPC, p2, 2/1 RPC, p2; rep from *, end p2, 2/1 LPC, p2

Rows 9 and 15: K2, p2, k3, *k3, p2, k2, p2, k3; rep from *, end k3, p2, k2

Row 10: P1, 2/1 RPC, p3, *p3, 2/1 LPC, 2/1 RPC, p3; rep from *, end p3, 2/1 LPC, p1

Rows 11 and 13: K1, p2, k4, *k4, p4, k4; rep from *, end k4, p2, k1

Row 12: P1, k2, p4, *p4, 2/2 RC, p4; rep from *, end p4, k2, p1

Row 14: P1, 2/1 LPC, p3, *p3, 2/1 RPC, 2/1 LPC, p3; rep from *, end p3, 2/1 RPC, p1

Row 16: P2, 2/1 LPC, p2, *p2, 2/1 RPC, p2, 2/1 LPC, p2; rep from *, end p2, 2/1 RPC, p2

Row 18: P3, 2/1 LPC, p1, *p1, 2/1 RPC, p4, 2/1 LPC, p1; rep from *, end p1, 2/1 RPC, p3

Row 20: P4, 2/1 LPC, *2/1 RPC, p6, 2/1 LPC; rep from *, end 2/1 RPC, p4

Variation: Isolate one multiple of pattern 3.8 to form a single diamond panel.

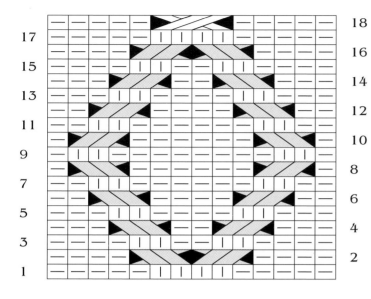

Panel of 14 stitches

Rows 1 and 17 (WS): K5, p4, k5
Row 2: P4, 2/1 RPC, 2/1 LPC, p4
Rows 3 and 15: K4, p2, k2, p2, k4
Row 4: P3, 2/1 RPC, p2, 2/1 LPC, p3
Rows 5 and 13: K3, p2, k4, p2, k3
Row 6: P2, 2/1 RPC, p4, 2/1 LPC, p2
Rows 7 and 11: K2, p2, k6, p2, k2
Row 8: P1, 2/1 RPC, p6, 2/1 LPC, p1
Row 9: K1, p2, k8, p2, k1
Row 10: P1, 2/1 LPC, p6, 2/1 RPC, p1
Row 12: P2, 2/1 LPC, p4, 2/1 RPC, p2
Row 14: P3, 2/1 LPC, p2, 2/1 RPC, p3
Row 16: P4, 2/1 LPC, 2/1 RPC, p4
Row 18: P5, 2/2 RC, p5

Ideas for Further Exploration

1. Fill the centers of the trellis or diamonds with texture stitches.

2. Cross all 2/2 crosses in the trellis pattern in the same direction—either right or left—instead of alternating the direction.

3. Elongate the trellis or diamond by working additional 2/2 crosses at the points where the cable ribs meet and cross.

Pattern 3.9: The use of 2/1 right and left crosses allows for the formation of braids. Braids differ from plaits in that 1) they may have more than three strands, and 2) those strands cross not only each other but may also cross background stitches (usually reverse stockinette stitch).

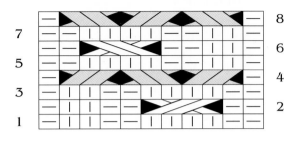

Panel of 11 stitches

Row 1 (WS): K1, p2, k2, p4, k2
Row 2: P2, 2/2 RC, p2, k2, p1
Row 3: K1, p2, k2, p4, k2
Row 4: P1, 2/1 RPC, 2/1 LPC, 2/1 RPC, p1
Row 5: K2, p4, k2, p2, k1
Row 6: P1, k2, p2, 2/2 LC, p2
Row 7: K2, p4, k2, p2, k1
Row 8: P1, 2/1 LPC, 2/1 RPC, 2/1 LPC, p1

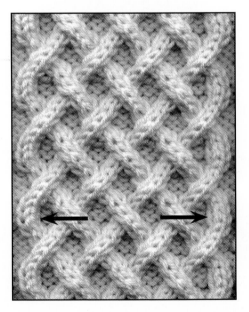

Variation #1: Repeating the braid, above, over an even number of knit ribs results in a balanced braid panel—that is, the outer knit ribs move out and in together.

Multiple of 6 stitches + 8

Row 1 (WS): K1, p2, k1, *k1, p4, k1; rep from *, end k1, p2, k1
Row 2: P1, k2, p1, *p1, 2/2 LC, p1; rep from *, end p1, k2, p1
Row 3: K1, p2, k1, *k1, p4, k1; rep from *, end k1, p2, k1
Row 4: P1, 2/1 LPC, *2/1 RPC, 2/1 LPC; rep from *, end 2/1 RPC, p1
Row 5: K2, p2, *p2, k2, p2; rep from *, end p2, k2
Row 6: P2, *2/2 RC, p2; rep from *, end 2/2 RC, p2
Row 7: K2, p2, *p2, k2, p2; rep from *, end p2, k2
Row 8: P1, 2/1 RPC, *2/1 LPC, 2/1 RPC; rep from *, end 2/1 LPC, p1

Variation #2: If the braid panel is worked with five knit ribs, the braid panel will be unbalanced—the outer knit ribs will move in and out alternately.

Multiple of 6 stitches + 11

Row 1 (WS): K1, p2, k2, *p4, k2; rep from *, end p4, k2

Row 2: P2, 2/2 RC, *p2, 2/2 RC; rep from *, end p2, k2, p1

Row 3: K1, p2, k2, *p4, k2; rep from *, end p4, k2

Row 4: P1, 2/1 RPC, *2/1 LPC, 2/1 RPC; rep from *, end 2/1 LPC, 2/1 RPC, p1

Row 5: K2, p4, k1, *k1, p4, k1; rep from *, end k1, p2, k1

Row 6: P1, k2, p1, *p1, 2/2 LC, p1; rep from *, end p1, 2/2 LC, p2

Row 7: K2, p4, k1, *k1, p4, k1; rep from *, end k1, p2, k1

Row 8: P1, 2/1 LPC, *2/1 RPC, 2/1 LPC; rep from *, end 2/1 RPC, 2/1 LPC, p1

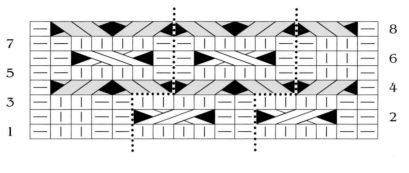

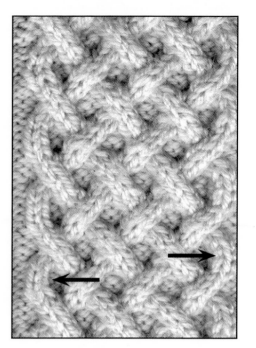

Ideas for Further Exploration

1. Expand these braid patterns by placing additional purl stitches between the knit ribs, making the knit ribs move farther across the purl background before meeting and crossing. (Hint: if you add enough purl stitches, you'll eventually end up with the trellis in pattern 3. 8)

2. Increase the number of times the knit ribs cross each other before traveling again.

1/1/1 Knit Crosses: Occasionally it is desirable to have the two outside stitches of a group of three change places, while the center stitch of the group stays where it is. In these versions, all stitches are knitted.

1/1/1 Right Cross

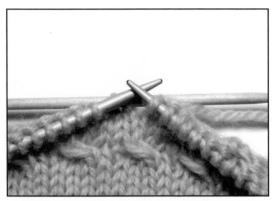

1. Slip the next two stitches to a cable needle and hold at the back of the work. Knit the next stitch from the left-hand needle.

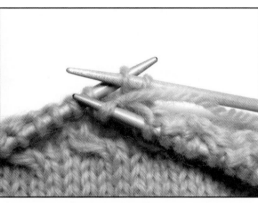

2. Slip the left-most stitch from the cable needle back to the left-hand needle and knit it.

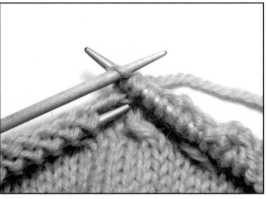

3. Knit the last stitch from the cable needle.

1/1/1 Left Cross

1. Slip the next two stitches to a cable needle and hold at the front of the work. Knit the next stitch from the left-hand needle.

2. Slip the left-most stitch from the cable needle back to the left-hand needle and knit it.

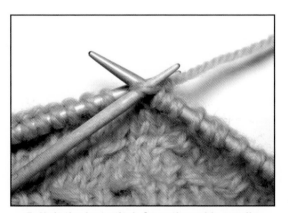

3. Knit the last stitch from the cable needle.

Pattern 3.10: Here, 1/1/1 right crosses are used on a stockinette background to create an allover spot pattern. The combination of crosses creates texture that resembles birds in flight.

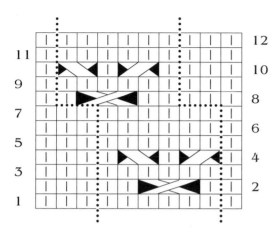

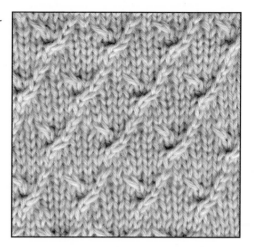

Multiple of 6 stitches + 4

Row 1 and all other WS rows: Purl
Row 2: K1, *k1, 1/1/1 RC, k2; rep from *, end k3
Row 4: K1, *1/1 RC, k1, 1/1 LC, k1; rep from *, end k3
Row 6: Knit
Row 8: K3, *k2, 1/1/1 RC, k1; rep from *, end k1
Row 10: K3, *k1, 1/1 RC, k1, 1/1 LC; rep from *, end k1
Row 12: Knit

Pattern 3.11: A simple twisting rope or wave cable is easy to work using the 1/1/1 right and left crosses. These are nice alternatives to the traditional four-stitch rope and wave cables. When repeated over a fabric, they make lovely ribbing patterns.

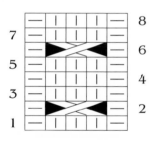

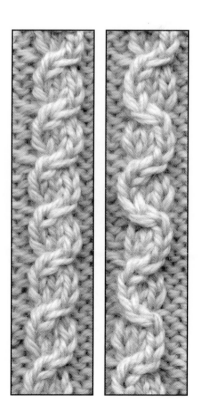

Panel of 5 stitches

Row 1 and all other WS rows: K1, p3, k1
Rows 2 and 6: P1, 1/1/1 RC, p1
Rows 4 and 8: P1, k3, p1

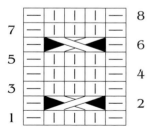

Panel of 5 stitches

Row 1 and all other WS rows: K1, p3, k1
Row 2: P1, 1/1/1 RC, p1
Rows 4 and 8: P1, k3, p1
Row 6: P1, 1/1/1 LC, p1

1/1/1 Reverse Cross: In this "inside-out" version of a 1/1/1 cross, the two outer knit stitches cross *behind* the central knit stitch.

1/1/1 Left Reverse Cross

1. Slip the next two stitches to a cable needle and hold at the front of the work.

2. Knit the next stitch from the left-hand needle.

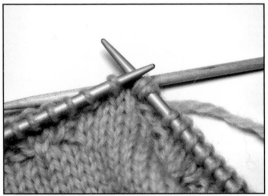

3. Slip the left-most stitch from the cable needle back to the left-hand needle. Pass the cable needle to the back of the work.

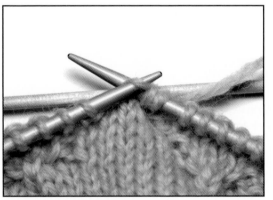

4. Knit the stitch which was slipped back to the left-hand needle.

5. Knit the stitch from the cable needle.

Pattern 3.12: A repeating pattern of 1/1/1 reverse crosses results in a fabric with a quilted or smocked appearance.

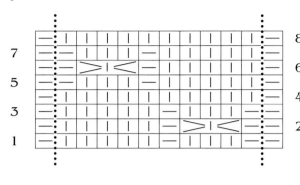

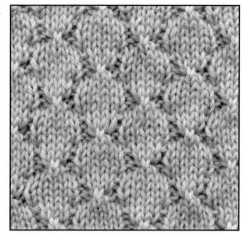

Multiple of 10 stitches + 2

Row 1 (WS): K1, *p5, k1, p3, k1; rep from *, end k1
Row 2: P1, *p1, 1/1/1 LRC, p1, k5; rep from *, end p1
Row 3: K1, *p5, k1, p3, k1; rep from *, end k1
Row 4: P1, *k10; rep from *, end p1
Row 5: K1, *k1, p3, k1, p5; rep from *, end k1
Row 6: P1, *k5, p1, 1/1/1 LRC, p1; rep from *, end p1
Row 7: K1, *k1, p3, k1, p5; rep from *, end k1
Row 8: P1, *k10; rep from *, end p1

Pattern 3.13: Here, the 1/1/1 reverse cross is used in a branching cable pattern; the branches "sprout" from the center knit stitch.

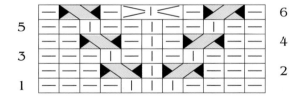

Panel of 11 stitches

Row 1 (WS): K4, p3, k4
Row 2: P3, 1/1 RPC, k1, 1/1 LPC, p3
Row 3: P3, (k1, p1) twice, k1, p3
Row 4: P2, 1/1 RPC, p1, k1, p1, 1/1 LPC, p2
Row 5: (K2, p1) three times, k2
Row 6: P1, 1/1 RPC, p1, 1/1/1 LRC, p1, 1/1 LPC, p1

1/1/1 Purl Crosses: Similar to 1/1/1 knit crosses, these cables are useful in situations where two knit stitches need to exchange places over a central purl stitch.

1/1/1 Right Purl Cross

1. Slip the next two stitches to a cable needle and hold at the back of the work.

2. Knit the next stitch from the left-hand needle.

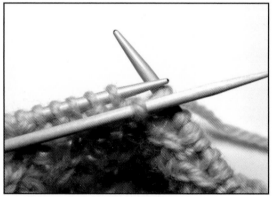

3. Slip the left-most stitch from the cable needle back to the left-hand needle, then bring the cable needle to the front of and to the left of that stitch.

4. Purl the stitch on the left-hand needle.

5. Knit the stitch from the cable needle.

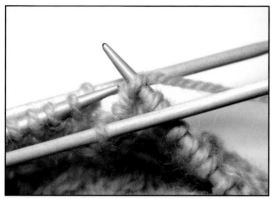

1. Slip the next stitch to a cable needle and hold at the front of the work. Slip the next stitch to a second cable needle and hold at the back of the work.

2. Knit the next stitch from the left-hand needle.

1/1/1 Left Purl Cross

3. Purl the stitch from the back cable needle.

4. Knit the stitch from the front cable needle.

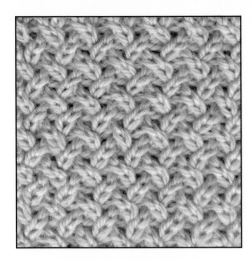

Pattern 3.14: Alternating 1/1/1 right and left purl crosses creates a delicate trellis pattern.

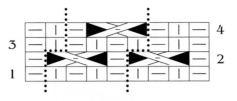

Multiple of 4 stitches + 5

Row 1 (WS): K1, *(p1, k1) twice; rep from *, end (p1, k1) twice
Row 2: P1, 1/1/1 LPC, *p1, 1/1/1 LPC; rep from *, end p1
Row 3: K1, p1, *(k1, p1) twice; rep from *, end k1, p1, k1
Row 4: P1, k1, p1, *1/1/1 RPC, p1; rep from *, end k1, p1

Pattern 3.15: Here, the 1/1/1 cross is used in a small, round cable pattern.

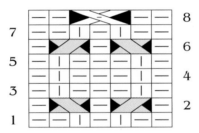

Panel of 7 stitches

Row 1 (WS): K2, p1, k1, p1, k2
Row 2: P1, 1/1 RPC, p1, 1/1 LPC, p1
Row 3: K1, p1, k3, p1, k1
Row 4: P1, k1, p3, k1, p1
Row 5: K1, p1, k3, p1, k1
Row 6: P1, 1/1 LPC, p1, 1/1 RPC, p1
Row 7: K2, p1, k1, p1, k2
Row 8: P2, 1/1/1 LPC, p2

Four-Stitch Crosses

Having looked through hundreds—if not thousands—of stitch patterns while preparing the material for this book, I believe I can safely say that four-stitch crosses are the most common kinds of cable crosses in cabling stitch patterns. This is the largest chapter in the book for a reason.

The possibilites for crossing combinations expands dramatically with this group: one stitch crossing over three, two stitches crossing over two, two outside stitches exchanging places over two central stitches, and three stitches crossing over one.

That last stitch combination—three stitches crossing over one—raises an important distinction. The cable patterns which feature ribs traveling back and forth across the background fabric fall into two categories: those with two knit stitches in the cable ribs and those with three stitches in the cable ribs. The latter are much "heavier" than the former. That characteristic can be used to advantage when planning a design— sometimes it is desirable to have a cable with a slightly heavier visual weight to it, which is where the cables with three-stitch ribs shine. As you look through this chapter and the ones to come, watch for those cables which have both two-stitch and three-stitch rib versions, and compare them.

1/3 Knit Crosses: These are not common crosses, but at least one cable stitch pattern relies on them.

1/3 Right Cross

1. Slip the next three stitches to a cable needle and hold at the back of the work.

2. Knit the next stitch from the left-hand needle.

3. Knit the three stitches from the cable needle.

1/3 Left Cross

1. Slip the next stitch to a cable needle and hold at the front of the work.

2. Knit the next three stitches from the left-hand needle.

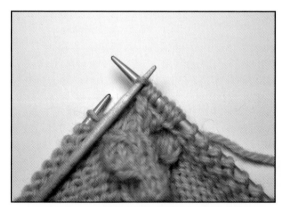

3. Knit the stitch from the cable needle.

Pattern 4.1: This horseshoe-style cable pattern is the only one that came to mind when looking for examples of 1/3 knit crosses, but it's a popular one. Depending upon the direction of the crosses, the horseshoe either cups up or down. It's often also seen with a small knot or bobble worked on the center knit stitch on row 4.

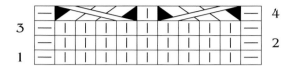
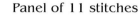

Panel of 11 stitches

Row 1 (WS): K1, p9, k1
Row 2: P1, k9, p1
Row 3: K1, p9, k1
Row 4: P1, 1/3 RC, k1, 1/3 LC, p1

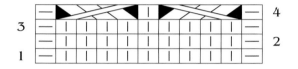

Panel of 11 stitches

Row 1 (WS): K1, p9, k1
Row 2: P1, k9, p1
Row 3: K1, p9, k1
Row 4: P1, 1/3 LC, k1, 1/3 RC, p1

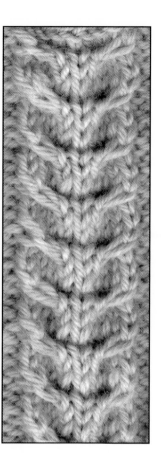

A note about 1/3 right and left purl crosses

I searched all of my stitch dictionaries—and I have several dozen—to find an example of a cable pattern featuring 1/3 right and left purl crosses. I could not find one. Interestingly, the symbols for 1/3 right and left purl crosses are included in the chart of 80 Basic Cable Crossings in Barbara Walker's *Charted Knitting Designs*. I can only assume that she included them (as well as the 1/4 right and left knit crosses) in the chart for completeness, as none of the cables in that volume use those crosses.

That doesn't mean that someone (maybe you?) won't design a cable using those crosses in the future. The sky is the limit when it comes to designing with cables.

2/2 Knit Crosses: These crosses form the basis of a huge number of popular cable stitch patterns.

2/2 Right Cross

1. Slip the next two stitches to a cable needle and hold at the back of the work.

2. Knit the next two stitches from the left-hand needle.

3. Knit the two stitches from the cable needle.

2/2 Left Cross

1. Slip the next two stitches to a cable needle and hold at the front of the work.

2. Knit the next two stitches from the left-hand needle.

3. Knit the two stitches from the cable needle.

Pattern 4.2: Placing 2/2 right and left crosses adjacent to each other creates a tight basketweave pattern. This is a very firm fabric and benefits from being worked on a needle size a bit larger than what might be recommended for the yarn.

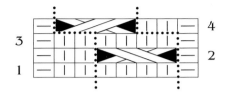

Multiple of 4 stitches + 4

Rows 1 and 3 (WS): K1, p2, *p4; rep from *, end, k1
Row 2: P1, *2/2 LC; rep from *, end k2, p1
Row 4: P1, k2, *2/2 RC; rep from *, end p1

Pattern 4.3: Here, 2/2 right and left crosses alternate to form a subtly-textured fabric. On row 2, 2/2 right crosses are spaced with four knit stitches. On row 6, the stitches which were knitted on row 2 become the stitches which are cabled, the stitches which are cabled, the stitches which were cabled on row 2 are knitted, and the cable changes to a 2/2 left cross.

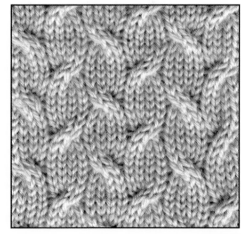

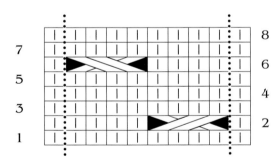

Multiple of 8 stitches + 2

Row 1 and all other WS rows: Purl
Row 2: K1, *2/2 RC, k4; rep from *, end k1
Row 4: Knit
Row 6: K1, *k4, 2/2 LC; rep from *, end k1
Row 8: Knit

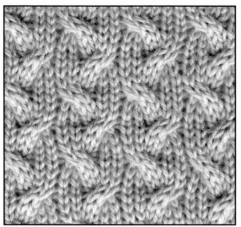

Pattern 4.4: This pattern is similar to pattern 4.3, except that the cables have been compressed later-ally—two of the stitches in the 2/2 RC of row 2 are also part of the 2/2 LC in row 6. Essentially, this is a series of braid cables placed side-by-side across the width of the fabric.

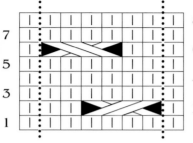

Multiple of 6 stitches + 2

Row 1 and all other WS rows: Purl
Row 2: K1, *2/2 RC, k2; rep from *, end k1
Row 4: Knit
Row 6: K1, *k2, 2/2 LC; rep from *, end k1
Row 8: Knit

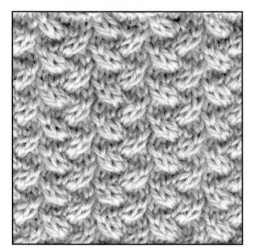

Variation #1: This is the same stitch pattern as the example in 4.4, except that the pattern has been com-pressed vertically. The cabling rows are separated by a single plain row, not three plain rows as in pattern 4.4.

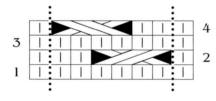

Multiple of 6 stitches + 2

Row 1 and all other WS rows: Purl
Row 2: K1, *2/2 RC, k2; rep from *, end k1
Row 4: K1, *k2, 2/2 LC; rep from *, end k1

Variation #2: The stitch pattern in pattern 4.4 forms the basis of this cable pattern, in which the basic cable pattern is mirror-imaged across the fabric, creating an entirely new stitch pattern.

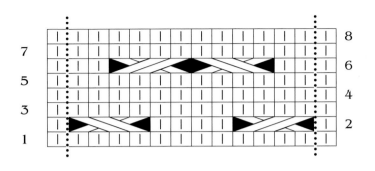

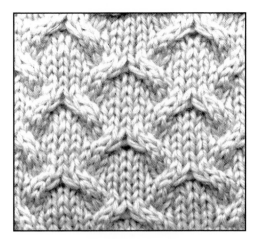

Multiple of 12 stitches + 2

Row 1 and all other WS rows: Purl
Row 2: K1, *2/2 RC, k4, 2/2 LC; rep from *, end k1
Row 4: Knit
Row 6: K1, *k2, 2/2 LC, 2/2 RC, k2; rep from *, end k1
Row 8: Knit

Ideas for Further Exploration

What other stockinette-based 2/2 right and left cross stitch patterns can you create? How does varying the number of plain rows between crosses, or the number of stitches between crosses, affect the gauge? How can you use that characteristic as a design feature?

Pattern 4.5: Isolating 2/2 right and left crosses and flanking them with purl stitches results in a group of cables quite familiar to many knitters. A 2/2 right or left cross repeated every four rows forms a rope cable, so-called because it does indeed resemble a rope.

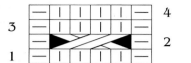

Panel of 6 stitches

Row 1 and all other WS rows: K1, p4, k1
Row 2: P1, 2/2 RC, p1
Row 4: P1, k4, p1

Panel of 6 stitches

Row 1 and all other WS rows: K1, p4, k1
Row 2: P1, 2/2 LC, p1
Row 4: P1, k4, p1

Variation #1: The rope cables can be made tighter or looser by varying the number of plain rows between cabling rows.

Panel of 6 stitches

Row 1 (WS): K1, p4, k1
Row 2: P1, 2/2 RC, p1

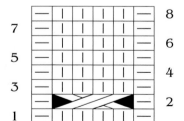

Panel of 6 stitches

Row 1 and all other WS rows: K1, p4, k1
Row 2: P1, 2/2 RC, p1
Rows 4, 6 and 8: P1, k4, p1

Variation #2: Alternate closely- and widely-spaced cable crossings.

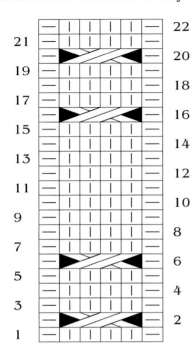

Panel of 6 stitches

Row 1 and all other WS rows: K1, p4, k1
Rows 2, 6, 16 and 20: P1, 2/2 RC, p1
Rows 4, 8, 10, 12, 14, 18 and 22: P1, k4, p1

Pattern 4.6: Alternating 2/2 left and right crosses changes a rope cable to a cable which resembles a wave moving back and forth.

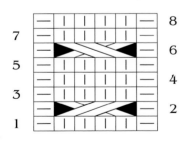

Panel of 6 stitches

Row 1 and all other WS rows: K1, p4, k1
Row 2: P1, 2/2 RC, p1
Rows 4 and 8: P1, k4, p1
Row 6: P1, 2/2 LC, p1

Pattern 4.7: Placing two 2/2 crosses adjacent to each other and crossing them in opposite directions forms a double cable, also known as a "horseshoe" cable because of its shape.

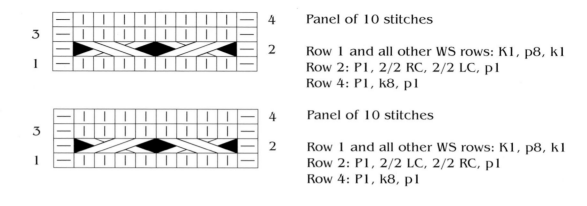

Panel of 10 stitches

Row 1 and all other WS rows: K1, p8, k1
Row 2: P1, 2/2 RC, 2/2 LC, p1
Row 4: P1, k8, p1

Panel of 10 stitches

Row 1 and all other WS rows: K1, p8, k1
Row 2: P1, 2/2 LC, 2/2 RC, p1
Row 4: P1, k8, p1

Variation #1: Widen the horseshoe by 4 additional stitches, and cross the top set of four stitches instead of simply allowing them to meet without crossing.

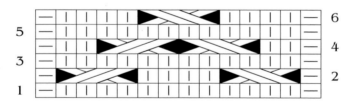

Panel of 14 stitches

Row 1 and all other WS rows: K1, p12, k1
Row 2: P1, 2/2 LC, k4, 2/2 RC, p1
Row 4: P1, k2, 2/2 LC, 2/2 RC, k2, p1
Row 6: P1, k4, 2/2 LC, k4, p1

Variation #2: Add two additional cabling rows, and move the crosses outward by two stitches each time. This stitch is often called a staghorn cable.

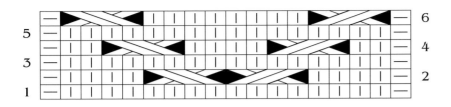

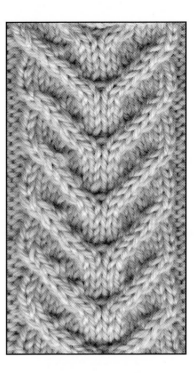

Panel of 18 stitches

Row 1 and all other WS rows: K1, p16, k1
Row 2: P1, k4, 2/2 RC, 2/2 LC, k4, p1
Row 4: P1, k2, 2/2 RC, k4, 2/2 LC, k2, p1
Row 6: P1, 2/2 RC, k8, 2/2 LC, p1

Variation #3: Make the following adjustments to pattern 4.7 for an even more interesting cable:

1. Work each cross twice.
2. Stagger the crosses.

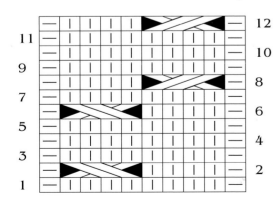

Panel of 10 stitches

Row 1 and all other WS rows: K1, p8, k1
Rows 2 and 6: P1, k4, 2/2 LC, p1
Rows 4 and 10: P1, k8, p1
Rows 8 and 12: P1, 2/2 RC, k4, p1

Pattern 4.8: Placing two 2/2 crosses adjacent to each other and crossing them alternately in and out forms the traditional "Aran Honeycomb" pattern.

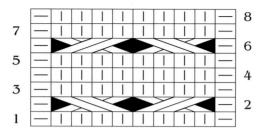

Panel of 10 stitches

Row 1 and all other WS rows: K1, p8, k1
Row 2: P1, 2/2 RC, 2/2 LC, p1
Rows 4 and 8: P1, k8, p1
Row 6: P1, 2/2 LC, 2/2 RC, p1

Variation #1: Lengthen the honeycomb by adding two non-cabling rows between the cabling rows.

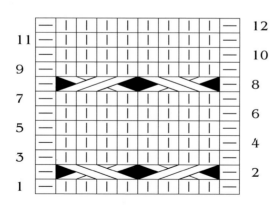

Panel of 10 stitches

Row 1 and all other WS rows: K1, p8, k1
Row 2: P1, 2/2 RC, 2/2 LC, p1
Rows 4, 6, 10 and 12: P1, k8, p1
Row 8: P1, 2/2 LC, 2/2 RC, p1

Variation #2: Separate the individual wave cables making up the honeycomb by one stitch (thus there will be an odd number of stitches between the strands), and fill the honeycomb with seed stitch or another texture stitch.

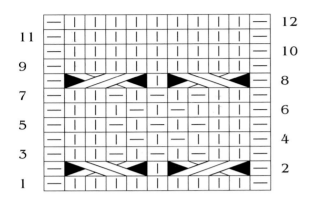

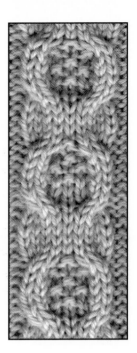

Panel of 11 stitches

Rows 1, 9 and 11 (WS): K1, p9, k1
Row 2: P1, 2/2 RC, k1, 2/2 LC, p1
Rows 3, 5 and 7: K1, p2, (k1, p1) twice, k1, p2, k1
Rows 4 and 6: P1, k3, (p1, k1) twice, k2, p1
Row 8: P1, 2/2 LC, k1, 2/2 RC, p1
Rows 10 and 12: P1, k9, p1

Ideas for Further Exploration

1. How can pattern 4.8 and its variations be used as wider panels or allover stitch patterns?

2. What other filler stitches might be used in the second variation of pattern 4.8?

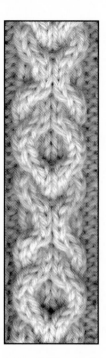

Pattern 4.9: Take pattern 4.8, double the row repeat, and alternate the directions of the crossings to create a cable which looks like a line of X's and O's.

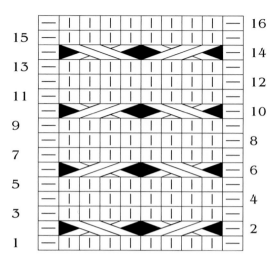

Panel of 10 stitches

Row 1 and all other WS rows: K1, p8, k1
Rows 2 and 14: P1, 2/2 RC, 2/2 LC, p1
Rows 4, 8, 12 and 16: P1, k8, p1
Rows 6 and 10: P1, 2/2 LC, 2/2 RC, p1

Variation: Expand the width of the cable, and move the cables in and out by two additional stitches on each side. Doing so makes a sharper version of pattern 4.9.

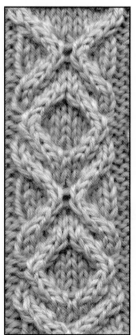

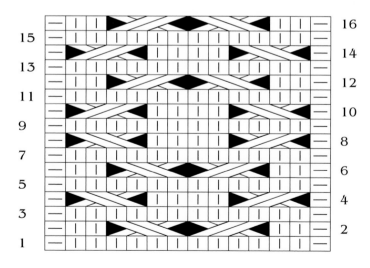

Panel of 14 stitches

Row 1 and all other WS rows: K1, p12, k1
Rows 2 and 6: P1, k2, 2/2 RC, 2/2 LC, k2, p1
Rows 4 and 8: P1, 2/2 RC, k4, 2/2 LC, p1
Rows 10 and 14: P1, 2/2 LC, k4, 2/2 RC, p1
Rows 12 and 16: P1, k2, 2/2 LC, 2/2 RC, k2, p1

Pattern 4.10: Braids are easy to form by alternating the directions of the crosses on alternate rows.

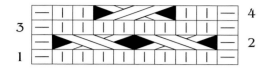

Panel of 10 stitches

Rows 1 and 3 (WS): K1, p8, k1
Row 2: P1, (2/2 LC) twice, p1
Row 4: P1, k2, 2/2 RC, k2, p1

2/2 Purl Crosses: Like their all-knit counterparts, this pair of crosses is seen frequently in many, many familiar cable stitch patterns.

2/2 Right Purl Cross

1. Slip the next two stitches to a cable needle and hold at the back of the work.

2. Knit the next two stitches from the left-hand needle.

3. Purl the two stitches from the cable needle.

2/2 Left Purl Cross

1. Slip the next two stitches to a cable needle and hold at the front of the work.

2. Purl the next two stitches from the left-hand needle.

3. Knit the two stitches from the cable needle.

Cables, Volume 1: The Basics

Pattern 4.11: In this pattern, 2/2 purl crosses are used to form zig-zagging lines.

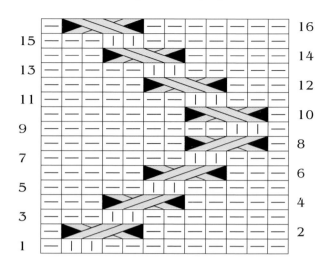

Panel of 12 stitches

Row 1 (WS): K1, p2, k9
Row 2: P7, 2/2 RC, p1
Row 3: K3, p2, k7
Row 4: P5, 2/2 RC, p3
Row 5: K5, p2, k5
Row 6: P3, 2/2 RC, p5
Row 7: K7, p2, k3
Row 8: P1, 2/2 RC, p7
Row 9: K9, p2, k1

Row 10: P1, 2/2 LC, p7
Row 11: K7, p2, k3
Row 12: P3, 2/2 LC, p5
Row 13: K5, p2, k5
Row 14: P5, 2/2 LC, p3
Row 15: K3, p2, k7
Row 16: P7, 2/2 LC, p1

Variation: A slightly looser and less angular line can be created by adding two non-cabling rows between rows 1 and 2 and between rows 8 and 9.

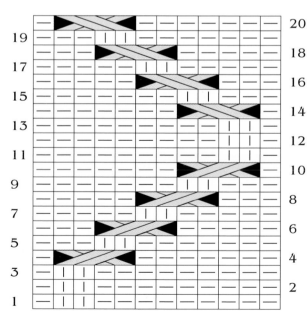

Panel of 12 stitches

Rows 1 and 3 (WS): K1, p2, k9
Row 2: P9, k2, p1
Row 4: P7, 2/2 RC, p1
Row 5: K3, p2, k7
Row 6: P5, 2/2 RC, p3
Row 7: K5, p2, k5
Row 8: P3, 2/2 RC, p5
Row 9: K7, p2, k3
Row 10: P1, 2/2 RC, p7
Rows 11 and 13: K9, p2, k1

Row 12: P1, k2, p9
Row 14: P1, 2/2 LC, p7
Row 15: K7, p2, k3
Row 16: P3, 2/2 LC, p5
Row 17: K5, p2, k5
Row 18: P5, 2/2 LC, p3
Row 19: K3, p2, k7
Row 20: P7, 2/2 LC, p1

Pattern 4.12: Here, two zig-zagging lines intertwine. Changing the 2/2 RC in row 28 to a 2/2 LC creates a pattern in which one line is always superimposed on top of the other line.

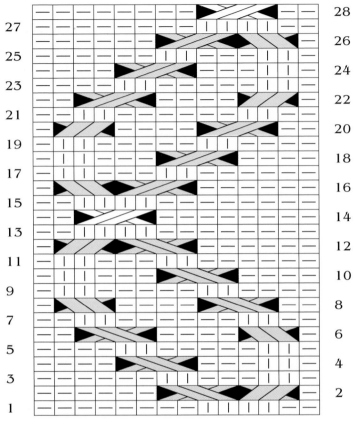

Panel of 14 stitches

Row 1 (WS): K8, p4, k2
Row 2: P1, 2/1 RPC, 2/2 LPC, p6
Row 3: K6, p2, k3, p2, k1
Row 4: P1, k2, p3, 2/2 LPC, p4
Row 5: K4, p2, k5, p2, k1
Row 6: P1, 2/1 LPC, p4, 2/2 LPC, p2
Row 7: K2, p2, k6, p2, k2
Row 8: P2, 2/2 LPC, p4, 2/1 LPC, p1
Row 9: K1, p2, k5, p2, k4
Row 10: P4, 2/2 LPC, p3, k2, p1
Row 11: K1, p2, k3, p2, k6
Row 12: P6, 2/2 LPC, 2/1 RPC, p1
Row 13: K2, p4, k8
Row 14: P8, 2/2 RC, p2
Row 15: K2, p4, k8
Row 16: P6, 2/2 RPC, 2/1 LPC, p1
Row 17: K1, p2, k3, p2, k6
Row 18: P4, 2/2 RPC, p3, k2, p1
Row 19: K1, p2, k5, p2, k4
Row 20: P2, 2/2 RPC, p4, 2/1 RPC, p1
Row 21: K2, p2, k6, p2, k2
Row 22: P1, 2/1 RPC, p4, 2/2 RPC, p2
Row 23: K4, p2, k5, p2, k1
Row 24: P1, k2, p3, 2/2 RPC, p4
Row 25: K6, p2, k3, p2, k1
Row 26: P1, 2/1 LPC, 2/2 RPC, p6
Row 27: K8, p4, k2
Row 28: P2, 2/2 RC, p8

Pattern 4.13: Zig-zagging lines which meet and cross form a trellis pattern.

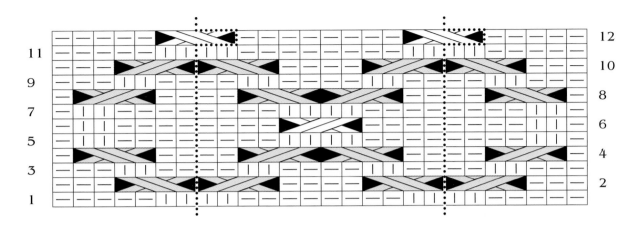

Multiple of 12 stitches + 14

Row 1 (WS): K5, p2, *p2, k8, p2; rep from *, end p2, k5
Row 2: P3, 2/2 RPC, *2/2 LPC, p4, 2/2 RPC; rep from *, end 2/2 LPC, p3
Row 3: K3, p2, k2, *k2, p2, k4, p2, k2; rep from *, end k2, p2, k3
Row 4: P1, 2/2 RPC, p2, *p2, 2/2 LPC, 2/2 RPC, p2; rep from *, end p2, 2/2 LPC, p1
Row 5: K1, p2, k4, *k4, p4, k4; rep from *, end k4, p2, k1
Row 6: P1, k2, p4, *p4, 2/2 RC, p4; rep from *, end p4, k2, p1
Row 7: K1, p2, k4, *k4, p4, k4; rep from *, end k4, p2, k1
Row 8: P1, 2/2 LPC, p2, *p2, 2/2 RPC, 2/2 LPC, p2; rep from *, end p2, 2/2 RPC, p1
Row 9: K3, p2, k2, *k2, p2, k4, p2, k2; rep from *, end k2, p2, k3
Row 10: P3, 2/2 LPC, *2/2 RPC, p4, 2/2 LPC; rep from *, end 2/2 RPC, p3
Row 11: K5, p2, *p2, k8, p2; rep from *, end p2, k5
Row 12: P5, *2/2 LC, p8; rep from *, end 2/2 LC, p5

Variation: Isolate one multiple of pattern 4.13 to form a single diamond panel. Note that this diamond is wider and squatter in appearance than the variation of pattern 3.8.

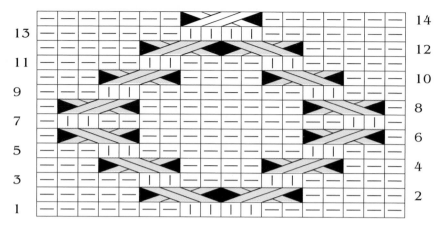

Panel of 18 stitches

Rows 1 and 13 (WS): K7, p4, k7
Row 2: P5, 2/2 RPC, 2/2 LPC, p5
Rows 3 and 11: K5, p2, k4, p2, k5
Row 4: P3, 2/2 RPC, p4, 2/2 LPC, p3
Rows 5 and 9: K3, p2, k8, p2, k3
Row 6: P1, 2/2 RPC, p8, 2/2 LPC, p1

Row 7: K1, p2, k12, p2, k1
Row 8: P1, 2/2 LPC, p8, 2/2 RPC, p1
Row 10: P3, 2/2 LPC, p4, 2/2 RPC, p3
Row 12: P5, 2/2 LPC, 2/2 RPC, p5
Row 14: P7, 2/2 RC, p7

Ideas for Further Exploration

1. Fill the centers of the trellis or diamonds with texture stitches.

2. Cross all 2/2 crosses in the trellis pattern in the same direction—either right or left—instead of alternating the direction.

Pattern 4.14: Alternately moving and crossing cable ribs forms this simple braid pattern. This 8-row man-uever forms the basis of many comon cable patterns, in which two-stitch ribs travel, cross, travel, and cross in the opposite direction. Interestingly, I have not seen this cable used as often as pattern 3.9.

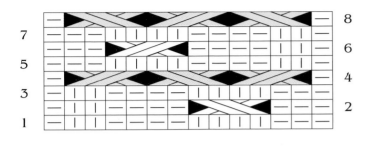

Panel of 14 stitches

Row 1 (WS): K1, p2, k4, p4, k3
Row 2: P3, 2/2 LC, p4, k2, p1
Row 3: K1, p2, k4, p4, k3
Row 4: P1, 2/2 RPC, 2/2 LPC, 2/2 RPC, p1
Row 5: K3, p4, k4, p2, k1
Row 6: P1, k2, p4, 2/2 RC, p3
Row 7: K3, p4, k4, p2, k1
Row 8: P1, 2/2 LPC, 2/2 RPC, 2/2 LPC, p1

Variation #1: Repeating the core 8 stitches of pattern 4.14 creates a wider braid panel.

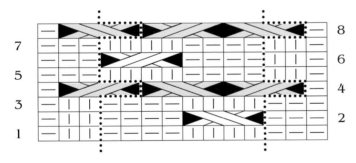

Multiple of 8 stitches + 6

Rows 1 and 3 (WS): K1, p2, *k4, p4; rep from *, end k3
Row 2: P3, *2/2 LC, p4; rep from *, end k2, p1
Row 4: P1, *2/2 RPC, 2/2 LPC; rep from *, end 2/2 RPC, p1
Rows 5 and 7: K3, *p4, k4; rep from *, end p2, k1
Row 6: P1, k2, *p4, 2/2 RC; rep from *, end p3
Row 8: P1, *2/2 LPC, 2/2 RPC; rep from *, end 2/2 LPC, p1

Variation #2: This is also a wide braid panel. Unlike the preceding variation, however, it is balanced—the outermost cable ribs move in and out in tandem instead of alternately.

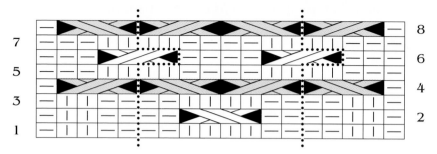

Multiple of 8 stitches + 10

Row 1 (WS): K1, p2, k2, *k2, p4, k2; rep from *, end k2, p2, k1
Row 2: P1, k2, p2, *p2, 2/2 LC, p2; rep from *, end p2, k2, p1
Row 3: K1, p2, k2, *k2, p4, k2; rep from *, end k2, p2, k1
Row 4: P1, 2/2 LPC, *2/2 RPC, 2/2 LPC; rep from *, end 2/2 RPC, p1
Row 5: K3, p2, *p2, k4, p2; rep from *, end p2, k3
Row 6: P3, *2/2 RC, p4; rep from *, end 2/2 RC, p3
Row 7: K3, p2, *p2, k4, p2; rep from *, end p2, k3
Row 8: P1, 2/2 RPC, *2/2 LPC, 2/2 RPC; rep from *, end 2/2 LPC, p1

Ideas for Further Exploration

1. How might cable 4.14 or its variations be expanded horizontally even further? What if it took four rows for the four-stitch cable sections to split, travel, and cross instead of just two? What would the cable look like?

2. Fill the open sections with bobbles or a filler stitch.

Variation #3: What happens when the braid from variation #2 is lengthened by an additional eight rows? The cable ribs travel, meet, and cross twice before traveling again. The number of times they cross can be increased to three or even four times.

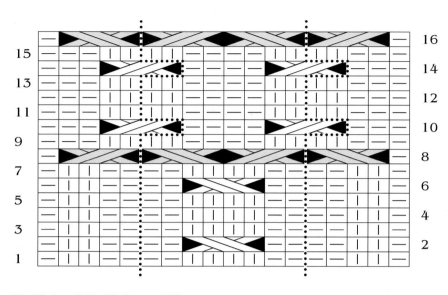

Multiple of 8 stitches + 10

Rows 1, 3, 5 and 7 (WS): K1, p2, k2, *k2, p4, k2; rep from *, end k2, p2, k1
Rows 2 and 6: P1, k2, p2, *p2, 2/2 LC, p2; rep from *, end p2, k2, p1
Row 4: P1, k2, p2, *p2, k4, p2; rep from *, end p2, k2, p1
Row 8: P1, 2/2 LPC, *2/2 RPC, 2/2 LPC; rep from *, end 2/2 RPC, p1
Rows 9, 11, 13 and 15: K3, p2, *p2, k4, p2; rep from *, end p2, k3
Rows 10 and 14: P3, *2/2 RC, p4; rep from *, end 2/2 RC, p3
Row 12: P3, k2, *k2, p4, k2; rep from *, end k2, p3
Row 16: P1, 2/2 RPC, *2/2 LPC, 2/2 RPC; rep from *, end 2/2 LPC, p1

Pattern 4.15: In this braid pattern, only two stitches of the four-stitch outer ribs move in and out as in variation #3 of pattern 4.14. The other two stitches continue in a straight vertical line. Furthermore, some of the ribs moving internally cross only once, not twice.

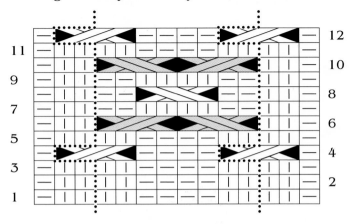

Multiple of 8 stitches + 6

Rows 1, 3, 5 and 11 (WS): K1, p2, *p2, k4, p2; rep from *, end p2, k1
Row 2: P1, k2, *k2, p4, k2; rep from *, end k2, p1
Rows 4 and 12: P1, 2/2 LC, *p4, 2/2 LC; rep from *, end p1
Row 6: P1, k2, *2/2 LPC, 2/2 RPC; rep from *, end k2, p1
Rows 7 and 9: K1, p2, *k2, p4, k2; rep from *, end p2, k1
Row 8: P1, k2, *p2, 2/2 LC, p2; rep from *, end k2, p1
Row 10: P1, k2, *2/2 RPC, 2/2 LPC; rep from *, end k2, p1

Pattern 4.16: Can you find the braid pattern within this cable stitch?

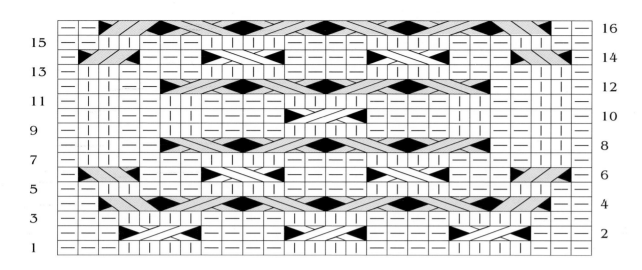

Panel of 26 sts

Row 1 (WS): K3, (p4, k4) twice, p4, k3
Row 2: P3, (2/2 RC, p4) twice, 2/2 RC, p3
Row 3: K3, (p4, k4) twice, p4, k3
Row 4: P2, 2/1 RPC, (2/2 LPC, 2/2 RPC) twice, 2/1 LPC, p2
Row 5: K2, p2, k3, p4, k4, p4, k3, p2, k2
Row 6: P1, 2/1 RPC, p3, 2/2 LC, p4, 2/2 LC, p3, 2/1 LPC, p1
Row 7: K1, p2, (k4, p4) twice, k4, p2, k1
Row 8: P1, k2, p2, (2/2 RPC, 2/2 LPC) twice, p2, k2, p1
Row 9: K1, p2, k2, p2, k4, p4, k4, p2, k2, p2, k1
Row 10: P1, k2, p2, k2, p4, 2/2 RC, p4, k2, p2, k2, p1
Row 11: K1, p2, k2, p2, k4, p4, k4, p2, k2, p2, k1
Row 12: P1, k2, p2, (2/2 LPC, 2/2 RPC) twice, p2, k2, p1
Row 13: K1, p2, (k4, p4) twice, k4, p2, k1
Row 14: P1, 2/1 LPC, p3, 2/2 LC, p4, 2/2 LC, p3, 2/1 RPC, p1
Row 15: K2, p2, k3, p4, k4, p4, k3, p2, k2
Row 16: P2, 2/1 LPC, (2/2 RPC, 2/2 LPC) twice, 2/1 RPC, p2

3/1 Knit Crosses: Here we have the first group of crosses that form the basis of visually-heavy cable stitch patterns.

3/1 Right Cross

1. Slip the next stitch to a cable needle and hold at the back of the work.

2. Knit the next three stitches from the left-hand needle.

3. Knit the stitch from the cable needle.

3/1 Left Cross

1. Slip the next three stitches to a cable needle and hold at the front of the work.

2. Knit the next stitch from the cable needle.

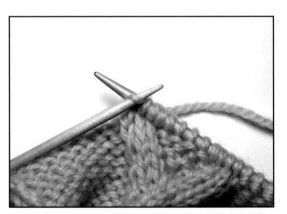

3. Knit the three stitches from the cable needle.

Pattern 4.17: Here, 3/1 crosses are used to form a "V"-shaped cable with garter stitch in the center. Compare it to pattern 3.4—the two are very similar in shape but not in size.

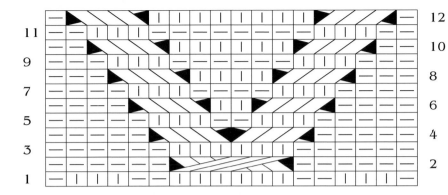

Panel of 18 sts

Row 1 (WS): K1, p3, k2, p6, k2, p3, k1
Row 2: P6, 3/3 RC, p6
Row 3: K6, p6, k6
Row 4: P5, 3/1 RC, 3/1 LC, p5
Row 5: K5, p3, k2, p3, k5
Row 6: P4, 3/1 RC, k2, 3/1 LC, p4
Row 7: K4, p3, k4, p3, k4
Row 8: P3, 3/1 RC, k4, 3/1 LC, p3
Row 9: K3, p3, k6, p3, k3
Row 10: P2, 3/1 RC, k6, 3/1 LC, p2
Row 11: K2, p3, k8, p3, k2
Row 12: P1, 3/1 RC, k8, 3/1 LC, p1

3/1 Purl Crosses: This group, like the preceeding one, is necessary to those cable stitch patterns which have three-stitch ribs instead of two-stitch ribs.

3/1 Right Purl Cross

1. Slip the next stitch to a cable needle and hold at the back of the work.

2. Knit the next three stitches from the left-hand needle.

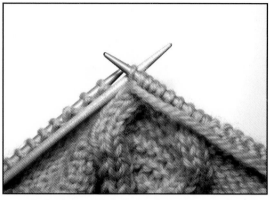

3. Purl the stitch from the cable needle.

3/1 Left Purl Cross

1. Slip the next three stitches to a cable needle and hold at the front of the work.

2. Purl the next stitch from the left-hand needle.

3. Knit the three stitches from the cable needle.

Pattern 4.18: This heavy traveling line is formed by moving 3/1 crosses travel back and forth across a purl background.

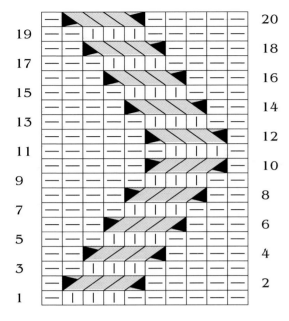

Panel of 10 sts

Row 1 (WS): K1, p3, k6
Row 2: P5, 3/1 RPC, p1
Row 3: K2, p3, k5
Row 4: P4, 3/1 RPC, p2
Row 5: K3, p3, k4
Row 6: P3, 3/1 RPC, p3
Row 7: K4, p3, k3
Row 8: P2, 3/1 RPC, p4
Row 9: K5, p3, k2
Row 10: P1, 3/1 RPC, p5
Row 11: K6, p3, k1
Row 12: P1, 3/1 LPC, p5
Row 13: K5, p3, k2
Row 14: P2, 3/1 LPC, p4
Row 15: K4, p3, k3
Row 16: P3, 3/1 LPC, p3
Row 17: K3, p3, k4
Row 18: P4, 3/1 LPC, p2
Row 19: K2, p3, k5
Row 20: P5, 3/1 LPC, p1

Ideas for Further Exploration

1. Add some textural elements, such as bobbles, on rows 2 and 12.

2. Make the traveling line less angular by adding two non-cabling rows between rows 10 and 12 and between rows 20 and 2.

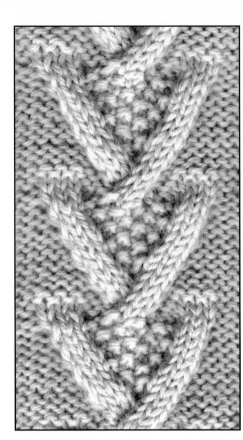

Pattern 4.19: Here, 3/1 knit and purl crosses are used to form a "V"-shaped cable with seed stitch in the center.

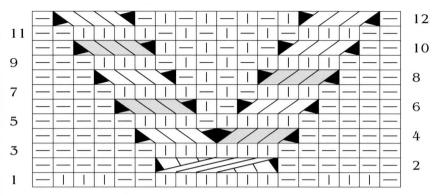

Panel of 18 sts

Row 1 (WS): K1, p3, k2, p6, k2, p3, k1
Row 2: P6, 3/3 RC, p6
Row 3: K6, p6, k6
Row 4: P5, 3/1 RPC, 3/1 LC, p5
Row 5: K5, p3, k1, p4, k5
Row 6: P4, 3/1 RC, p1, k1, 3/1 LPC, p4
Row 7: K4, p4, k1, p1, k1, p3, k4
Row 8: P3, 3/1 RPC, (k1, p1) twice, 3/1 LC, p3
Row 9: K3, p3, (k1, p1) three times, p3, k3
Row 10: P2, 3/1 RC, (p1, k1) three times, 3/1 LPC, p2
Row 11: K2, p3, (p1, k1) four times, p3, k2
Row 12: P1, 3/1 RC, (k1, p1) four times, 3/1 LC, p1

Pattern 4.20: Doubling the "V"-shaped cable vertically allows for the formation of diamonds. This one is filled with seed stitch, as in the previous pattern.

Panel of 18 sts

Row 1 (WS): K6, p6, k6
Row 2: P5, 3/1 RPC, 3/1 LC, p5
Row 3: K5, p3, k1, p4, k5
Row 4: P4, 3/1 RC, p1, k1, 3/1 LPC, p4
Row 5: K4, p4, k1, p1, k1, p3, k4
Row 6: P3, 3/1 RPC, (k1, p1) twice, 3/1 LC, p3
Row 7: K3, p3, (k1, p1) three times, p3, k3
Row 8: P2, 3/1 RC, (p1, k1) three times, 3/1 LPC, p2
Row 9: K2, p3, (p1, k1) four times, p3, k2
Row 10: P1, 3/1 RPC, (k1, p1) four times, 3/1 LC, p1
Row 11: K1, p3, (k1, p1) five times, p3, k1
Row 12: P1, 3/1 LPC, (k1, p1) four times, 3/1 RPC, p1
Row 13: K2, p3, (p1, k1) four times, p3, k2
Row 14: P2, 3/1 LPC, (p1, k1) three times, 3/1 RPC, p2
Row 15: K3, p3, (k1, p1) three times, p3, k3
Row 16: P3, 3/1 LPC, (k1, p1) twice, 3/1 RPC, p3
Row 17: K4, p3, (p1, k1) twice, p3, k4
Row 18: P4, 3/1 LPC, p1, k1, 3/1 RPC, p4
Row 19: K5, p3, k1, p4, k5
Row 20: P5, 3/1 LPC, 3/1 RPC, p5
Row 21: K6, p6, k6
Row 22: P6, 3/3 RC, p6

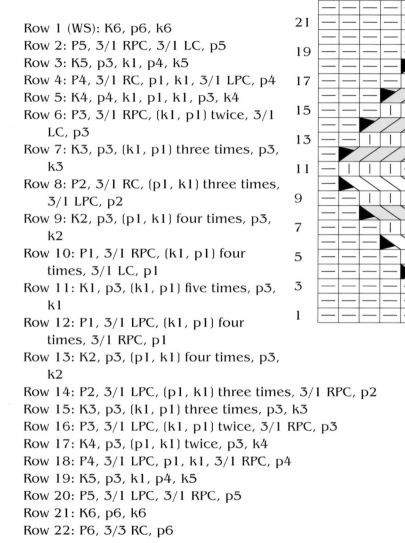

Pattern 4.21: Moving the traveling lines alternately in and out so that they meet and cross results in a braid pattern. This is somewhat similar to stitch pattern 4.13, except that the 2/2 right and left purl crosses have been replaced by 3/1 purl crosses, and the 2/2 knit crosses have been replaced by 3/3 knit crosses.

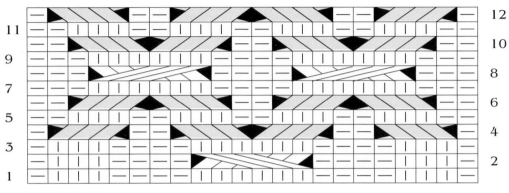

Panel of 22 stitches

Row 1 (WS): K1, p3, k4, p6, k4, p3, k1
Row 2: P1, k3, p4, 3/3 LC, p4, k3, p1
Row 3: K1, p3, k4, p6, k4, p3, k1
Row 4: P1, (3/1 LPC, p2, 3/1 RPC) twice, p1
Row 5: (K2, p3) four times, k2
Row 6: (P2, 3/1 LPC, 3/1 RPC) twice, p2

Row 7: K3, p6, k4, p6, k3
Row 8: P3, 3/3 RC, p4, 3/3 RC, p3
Row 9: K3, p6, k4, p6, k3
Row 10: (P2, 3/1 RPC, 3/1 LPC) twice, p2
Row 11: (K2, p3) four times, k2
Row 12: P1, (3/1 LPC, p2, 3/1 RPC) twice, p1

Ideas for Further Exploration

Which other cable stitches featuring two-stitch ribs have versions featuring three-stitch ribs? If a three-stitch rib version doesn't exist, how could you design one?

Variation: Look carefully—this is the same stitch pattern as 4.21, with a few changes: The row repeat has been doubled to 24 rows, and some all-knit crosses have changed direction so that one pair of ribs is superimposed over the other.

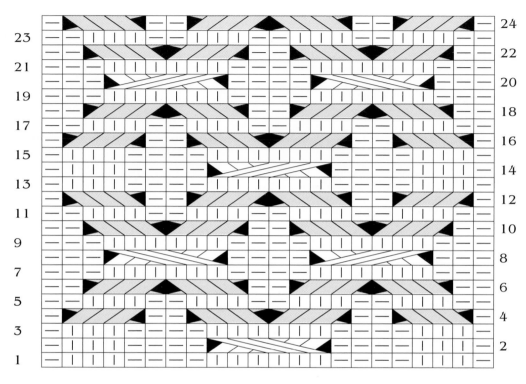

Panel of 22 sts

Rows 1, 3, 13 and 15 (WS): K1, p3, k4, p6, k4, p3, k1

Row 2: P1, k3, p4, 3/3 LC, p4, k3, p1

Row 4: P1, (3/1 LPC, p2, 3/1 RPC) twice, p1

Rows 5, 11, 17 and 23: (K2, p3) four times, k2

Row 6: (P2, 3/1 LPC, 3/1 RPC) twice, p2

Rows 7, 9, 19 and 21: K3, p6, k4, p6, k3

Row 8: P3, 3/3 RC, p4, 3/3 LC, p3

Row 10: (P2, 3/1 RPC, 3/1 LPC) twice, p2

Row 12: P1, (3/1 RPC, p2, 3/1 LPC) twice, p1

Row 14: P1, k3, p4, 3/3 RC, p4, k3, p1

Row 16: P1, (3/1 LPC, p2, 3/1 RPC) twice, p1

Row 18: (P2, 3/1 LPC, 3/1 RPC) twice, p2

Row 20: P3, 3/3 LC, p4, 3/3 RC, p3

Row 22: (P2, 3/1 RPC, 3/1 LPC) twice, p2

Row 24: P1, (3/1 RPC, p2, 3/1 LPC) twice, p1

1/2/1 Knit Crosses: This is an unusual set of crosses in which the outermost knit stitches exchange places over two stationary center stitches. In this version, all stitches are knitted.

1/2/1 Right Cross

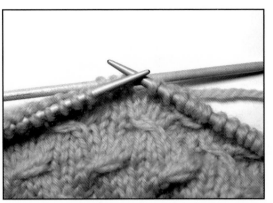

1. Slip the next three stitches to a cable needle and hold at the back of the work.

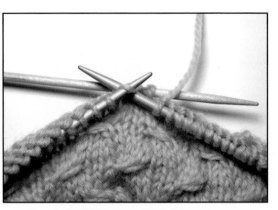

2. Knit the next stitch from the left-hand needle.

3. Slip the two left-most stitches from the cable needle back to the left-hand needle and knit them.

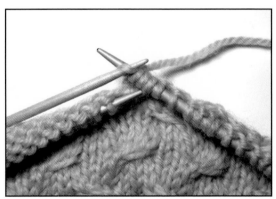

4. Knit the stitch from the cable needle.

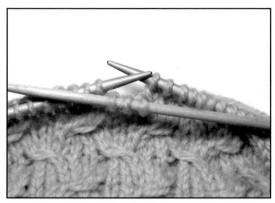

1. Slip the next three stitches to a cable needle and hold at the front of the work.

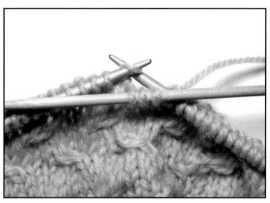

2. Knit the next stitch from the left-hand needle.

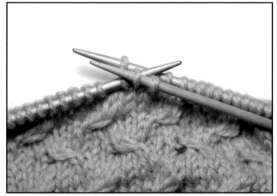

3. Slip the two left-most stitches from the cable needle back to the left-hand needle and knit them.

4. Knit the stitch from the cable needle.

1/2/1 Left Cross

Pattern 4.22: Here, an alternating pattern of right and left 1/2/1 crosses forms a delicate allover pattern.

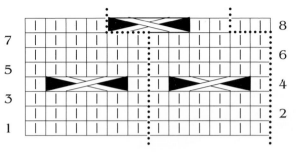

Multiple of 6 stitches + 6

Row 1 and all other WS rows: Purl
Rows 2 and 6: Knit
Row 4: *K1, 1/2/1 RC, k1; rep from *, end k1, 1/2/1 RC, k1
Row 8: K2, *k2, 1/2/1 LC; rep from *, end k4

1/2/1 Purl Crosses: This set of crosses is identical to the previous set except that the two stationary center stitches are purls instead of knits, and the crossings are made in such a way that those two purl stitches remain at the back of the fabric.

1. Slip the next three stitches to a cable needle and hold at the back of the work.

2. Knit the next stitch from the left-hand needle.

1/2/1 Right Purl Cross

3. Slip the two left-most stitches from the cable needle back to the left-hand needle, then bring the cable needle to the front and to the left of those stitches.

4. Purl the two stitches from the left-hand needle.

5. Knit the stitch from the cable needle.

1/2/1 Left Purl Cross

1. Slip the next stitch to a cable needle and hold at the front of the work. Slip the following two stitches to a second cable needle and hold at the back of the work.

2. Knit the next stitch from the left-hand needle.

3. Purl the two stitches from the back cable needle.

4. Knit the stitch from the front cable needle.

Pattern 4.23: A delicate trellis pattern is formed when 1/2/1 right and left purl crosses combine across the fabric.

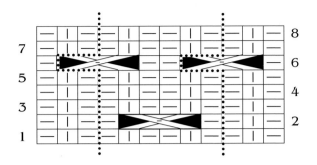

Multiple of 6 stitches + 6

Row 1 and all other WS rows: K1, p1, k1, *k1, p1, k2, p1, k1; rep from *, end k1, p1, k1
Row 2: P1, k1, p1, *p1, 1/2/1 LC, p1; rep from *, end p1, k1, p1
Rows 4 and 8: P1, k1, p1, *p1, k1, p2, k1, p1; rep from *, end p1, k1, p1
Row 6: P1, 1/2/1 RC, *p2, 1/2/1 RC; rep from *, end p1

Five-Stitch Crosses

Our trip through the Land of Cables is about to leave the popular tourist destinations to explore some lesser-known areas. In this and the following three chapters, the emphasis won't be so much on the relationships between the cable stitch patterns and how they evolved from each other; rather, these chapters will concentrate on the unique features of their groups of stitches.

The five-stitch crosses are an interesting group. They aren't called upon often, but when it's necessary to cross an odd-numbered group of stitches a specific way, they step in and fill the need. This group has a number of fascinating combinations: two stitches over three, three stitches over two, four stitches over one, two outside stitches exchanging places over three central stitches, and four outside stitches exchanging places over a central stitch.

2/3 Knit Crosses

2/3 Right Cross

1. Slip the next three stitches to a cable needle and hold at the back of the work.

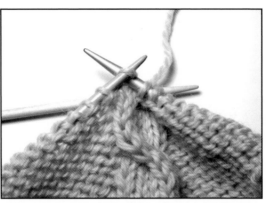

2. Knit the next two stitches from the left-hand needle.

3. Knit the three stitches from the cable needle.

2/3 Left Cross

1. Slip the next two stitches to a cable needle and hold at the front of the work.

2. Knit the next three stitches from the left-hand needle.

3. Knit the two stitches from the cable needle.

Pattern 5.1: In this interesting variation on a wave cable, a two-stitch rib crosses back and forth over a three-stitch garter background.

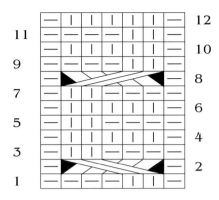

Panel of 7 stitches

Row 1 (WS): K4, p2, k1
Row 2: P1, 2/3 LC, p1
Row 3: K1, p2, k4
Row 4: P1, k5, p1
Row 5: K1, p2, k4
Row 6: P1, k5, p1
Row 7: K1, p2, k4
Row 8: P1, 2/3 RC, p1
Row 9: K4, p2, k1
Row 10: P1, k5, p1
Row 11: K4, p2, k1
Row 12: P1, k5, p1

Ideas for Further Exploration

Mirror-image this pattern and repeat it across a larger number of stitches to form a central panel.

Pattern 5.2: Here is an excellent example of a situation where a five-stitch cross is preferable to a four-stitch cross. This pattern is similar to pattern 4.20, except that the center of the cable has an odd, not an even, number of stitches. Use this cross when you wish to fill the center of this kind of cable with a filler stitch based on an odd number of stitches—such as seed or rice stitch—or with a bobble, which must be centered on an odd number of stitches.

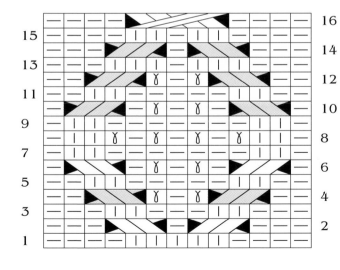

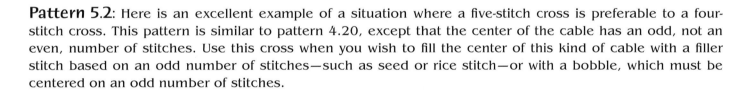

Panel of 13 stitches

Row 1 (WS): K4, p5, k4
Row 2: P3, 2/1 RC, p1, 2/1 LC, p3
Row 3 and 13: (K3, p2) twice, k3
Row 4: P2, 2/1 RPC, k1tbl, p1, k1tbl, 2/1 LPC, p2
Rows 5 and 11: K2, p2, k5, p2, k2
Row 6: P1, 2/1 RC, (p1, k1tbl) twice, p1, 2/1 LC, p1
Rows 7 and 9: K1, p2, k7, p2, k1
Row 8: P1, k2, (k1tbl, p1) three times, k1tbl, k2, p1
Row 10: P1, 2/1 LPC, (p1, k1tbl) twice, p1, 2/1 RPC, p1
Row 12: P2, 2/1 LPC, k1tbl, p1, k1tbl, 2/1 RPC, p2
Row 14: P3, 2/1 LPC, p1, 2/1 RPC, p3
Row 15: K4, p2, k1, p2, k4
Row 16: P4, 2/3 RC, p4

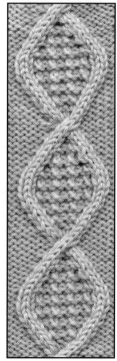

2/3 Purl Crosses

2/3 Right Purl Cross

1. Slip the next three stitches to a cable needle and hold at the back of the work.

2. Knit the next two stitches from the left-hand needle.

3. Purl the three stitches from the cable needle.

2/3 Left Purl Cross

1. Slip the next two stitches to a cable needle and hold at the front of the work.

2. Purl the next three stitches from the left-hand needle.

3. Knit the two stitches from the cable needle.

Pattern 5.3: In this example, 2/3 purl crosses perfectly meet a need. They are required to form the top and bottom of a large rounded cable. If 2/2 purl crosses were used here instead, the circle would have more of an elliptical than round shape.

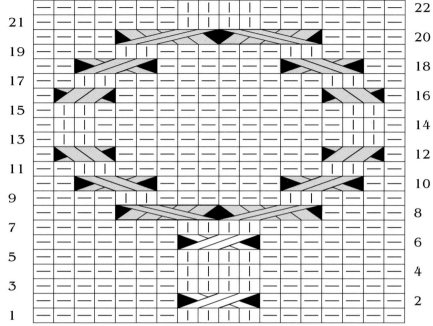

Panel of 18 sts

Rows 1, 3, 5 and 7 (WS): K7, p4, k7
Rows 2 and 6: P7, 2/2 RC, p7
Row 4: P7, k4, p7
Row 8: P4, 2/3 RPC, 2/3 LPC, p4
Row 9: K4, p2, k6, p2, k4
Row 10: P2, 2/2 RPC, p6, 2/2 LPC, p2
Row 11: K2, p2, k10, p2, k2
Row 12: P1, 2/1 RPC, p10, 2/1 LPC, p1
Row 13: K1, p2, k12, p2, k1
Row 14: P1, k2, p12, k2, p1
Row 15: K1, p2, k12, p2, k1
Row 16: P1, 2/1 LPC, p10, 2/2 RPC, p1
Row 17: K2, p2, k10, p2, k2
Row 18: P2, 2/2 LPC, p6, 2/2 RPC, p2
Row 19: K4, p2, k6, p2, k4
Row 20: P4, 2/3 LPC, 2/3 RPC, p4
Row 21: K7, p4, k7
Row 22: P7, k4, p7

Ideas for Further Exploration

1. Fill the circle with seed, moss, or some other filler stitch.

2. Place two of these cables next to each other and "interlock" them by crossing them on row 14 when they meet.

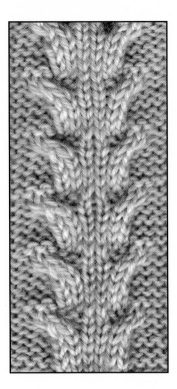

Pattern 5.4: Another good use of 2/3 purl crosses is in this stitch pattern. Moving the knit stitches from the center of the pattern out to the sides forms a textured branching shape. Note that some of the stitches which were knitted on row 7 are purled on row 8, and vice-versa.

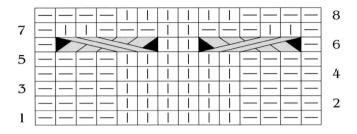

Panel of 14 stitches

Rows 1, 3 and 5 (WS): K4, p6, k4
Rows 2 and 4: P4, k6, p4
Row 6: P1, 2/3 RPC, k2, 2/3 LPC, p1
Row 7: K1, (p2, k3) twice, p2, k1
Row 8: P4, k6, p4

3/2 Knit Crosses

3/2 Right Cross

1. Slip the next two stitches to a cable needle and hold at the back of the work.

2. Knit the next three stitches from the left-hand needle.

3. Knit the two stitches from the cable needle.

3/2 Left Cross

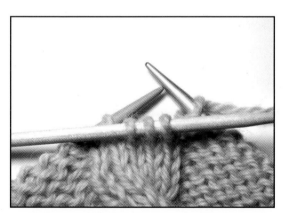

1. Slip the next three stitches to a cable needle and hold at the front of the work.

2. Knit the next two stitches from the left-hand needle.

3. Knit the three stitches from the cable needle.

Pattern 5.5: Barbara Walker notes in *A Treasury of Knitting Patterns* that "(l)ong ago all cables were worked on uneven stitches, the larger number of stitches being crossed in front and a smaller number behind." Here is an example of such a cable: three stitches cross over two to form a rope cable. The same concept could be applied to a wave cable over five stitches.

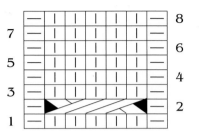

Panel of 7 stitches

Row 1 and all other WS rows: K1, p5, k1
Row 2: P1, 3/2 RC, p1
Rows 4, 6 and 8: P1, k5, p1

Ideas for Further Exploration

Do you see a noticeable difference between this version of rope cable and the standard version? In what situations might this version be preferable?

3/2 Purl Crosses

3/2 Right Purl Cross

1. Slip the next two stitches to a cable needle and hold at the back of the work.

2. Knit the next three stitches from the left-hand needle.

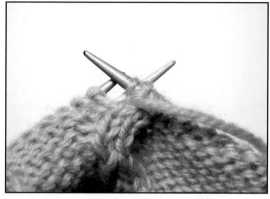

3. Purl the two stitches from the cable needle.

3/2 Left Purl Cross

1. Slip the next three stitches to a cable needle and hold at the front of the work.

2. Purl the next two stitches from the left-hand needle.

3. Knit the three stitches from the cable needle.

Pattern 5.6: In this stitch pattern, the 2/3 crosses are used to simulate "threading" of the cable ribs. This is a fascinating pattern and an excellent use of 2/3 and 3/2 crosses.

Multiple of 34 stitches + 8

Rows 1 and 3 (WS): K1, p3, *p3, k4, p6, k8, p6, k4, p3; rep from *, end p3, k1
Row 2: P1, *3/3 LC, p4, k6, p8, k6, p4; rep from *, end 3/3 LC, p1
Row 4: P1, k3, *3/2 LPC, p2, k6, p8, k6, p2, 3/2 RPC; rep from *, end k3, p1
Rows 5 and 31: K1, p3, *k2, p3, k2, p6, k8, p6, k2, p3, k2; rep from *, end p3, k1
Row 6: P1, k3, *p2, 3/2 LPC, k6, p8, k6, 3/2 RPC, p2; rep from *, end k3, p1
Rows 7, 9, 11, 13, 23, 25, 27 and 29: K1, p3, *k4, p9, k8, p9, k4; rep from *, end p3, k1
Row 8: P1, k3, *p4, 2/3 RC, k4, p8, k4, 3/2 RC, p4; rep from *, end k3, p1
Row 10: P1, k3, *p4, k2, 3/2 LC, k2, p8, k2, 2/3 LC, k2, p4; rep from *, end k3, p1
Row 12: P1, k3, *p4, k4, 2/3 RC, p8, 3/2 RC, k4, p4; rep from *, end k3, p1
Row 14: P1, k3, *p4, k6, 3/2 LPC, p4, 3/2 RPC, k6, p4; rep from *, end k3, p1
Rows 15 and 21: K1, p3, *k4, p6, k2, p3, k4, p3, k2, p6, k4; rep from *, end p3, k1
Row 16: P1, k3, *p4, k6, p2, 3/2 LPC, 3/2 RPC, p2, k6, p4; rep from *, end k3, p1
Rows 17 and 19: K1, p3, *(k4, p6) three times, k4; rep from *, end p3, k1
Row 18: P1, k3, *p4, k6, p4, 3/3 LC, p4, k6, p4; rep from *, end k3, p1
Row 20: P1, k3, *p4, k6, p2, 3/2 RPC, 3/2 LPC, p2, k6, p4; rep from *, end k3, p1
Row 22: P1, k3, *p4, k6, 3/2 RPC, p4, 3/2 LPC, k6, p4; rep from *, end k3, p1
Row 24: P1, k3, *p4, k4, 3/2 RC, p8, 2/3 RC, k4, p4; rep from *, end k3, p1
Row 26: P1, k3, *p4, k2, 2/3 LC, k2, p8, k2, 3/2 LC, k2, p4; rep from *, end k3, p1
Row 28: P1, k3, *p4, 3/2 RC, k4, p8, k4, 2/3 RC, p4; rep from *, end k3, p1
Row 30: P1, k3, *p2, 3/2 RPC, k6, p8, k6, 3/2 LPC, p2; rep from *, end k3, p1
Row 32: P1, k3, *3/2 RPC, p2, k6, p8, k6, p2, 3/2 LPC; rep from *, end k3, p1

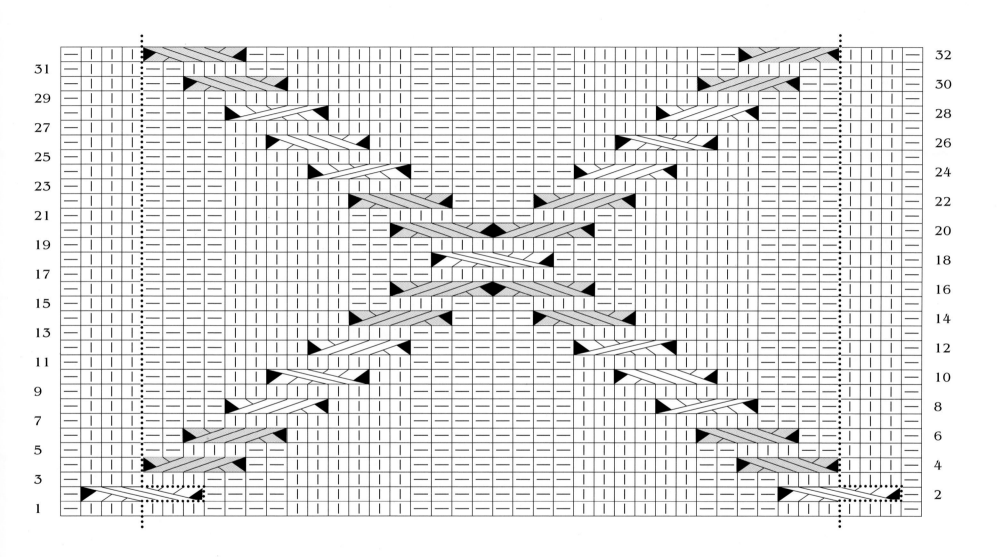

Pattern 5.7: With this stitch pattern we again see how a column of stitches—in this case, one which is three stitches wide—can be made to travel back and forth over background stitches.

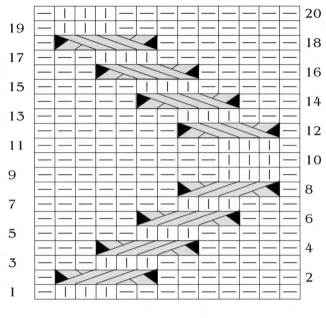

Panel of 13 stitches

Row 1 (WS): K1, p3, k9
Row 2: P7, 3/2 RPC, p1
Row 3: K3, p3, k7
Row 4: P5, 3/2 RPC, p3
Row 5: K5, p3, k5
Row 6: P3, 3/2 RPC, p5
Row 7: K7, p3, k3
Row 8: P1, 3/2 RPC, p7
Row 9: K9, p3, k1
Row 10: P1, k3, p9
Row 11: P9, k3, p1
Row 12: P1, 3/2 LPC, p7
Row 13: K7, p3, k3
Row 14: P3, 3/2 LPC, p5
Row 15: K5, p3, k5
Row 16: P5, 3/2 LPC, p3
Row 17: K3, p3, k7
Row 18: P7, 3/2 LPC, p1
Row 19: K1, p3, k9
Row 20: P9, k3, p1

Ideas for Further Exploration

What accents might be added to this traveling line? How else might it be varied?

Pattern 5.8: This stitch pattern is an bigger version of stitch pattern 4.12. Here, the traveling lines are composed of three stitches, and one rib is completely superimposed over the other.

Panel of 16 stitches

Row 1 (WS): K8, p6, k2
Row 2: P2, 3/3 LC, p8
Row 3: K8, p6, k2
Row 4: P1, 3/1 RPC, 3/2 LPC, p6
Row 5: K6, p3, k3, p3, k1
Row 6: P1, k3, p3, 3/2 LPC, p4
Row 7: K4, p3, k5, p3, k1
Row 8: P1, 3/1 LPC, p4, 3/2 LPC, p2
Row 9: K2, p3, k6, p3, k2
Row 10: P2, 3/2 LPC, p4, 3/1 LPC, p1
Row 11: K1, p3, k5, p3, k4
Row 12: P4, 3/2 LPC, p3, k3, p1
Row 13: K1, p3, k3, p3, k6
Row 14: P6, 3/2 LPC, 3/1 RPC, p1
Row 15: K2, p6, k8
Row 16: P8, 3/3 RC, p2
Row 17: K2, p6, k8
Row 18: P6, 3/2 RPC, 3/1 LPC, p1
Row 19: K1, p3, k3, p3, k6
Row 20: P4, 3/2 RPC, p3, k3, p1
Row 21: K1, p3, k5, p3, k4
Row 22: P2, 3/2 RPC, p4, 3/1 RPC, p1
Row 23: K2, p3, k6, p3, k2
Row 24: P1, 3/1 RPC, p4, 3/2 RPC, p2
Row 25: K4, p3, k5, p3, k1
Row 26: P1, k3, p3, 3/2 RPC, p4
Row 27: K6, p3, k3, p3, k1
Row 28: P1, 2/1 LPC, 3/2 RPC, p6

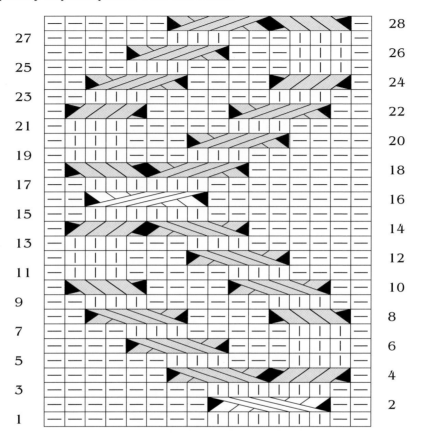

1/3/1 Knit Crosses

1/3/1 Right Cross

1. Slip the next four stitches to a cable needle and hold at the back of the work.

2. Knit the next stitch from the left-hand needle.

3. Slip the three left-most stitches from the cable needle back to the left-hand needle and knit them.

4. Knit the stitch from the cable needle.

1/3/1 Left Cross

1. Slip the next four stitches to a cable needle and hold at the front of the work.

2. Knit the next stitch from the left-hand needle.

3. Slip the three left-most stitches from the cable needle back to the left-hand needle and knit them.

4. Knit the stitch from the cable needle.

Pattern 5.9: Interesting effects can now be achieved by having the two outer stitches exchange places while the three inner stitches remain where they are. This cross allows for the creation of a nicely rounded small cable.

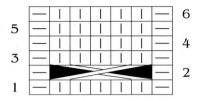

Panel of 7 sts

Row 1 and all other WS rows: K1, p5, k1
Row 2: P1, 1/3/1 RC, p1
Rows 4 and 6: P1, k5, p1

Variation: Fill the center of the circle with seed stitch or some other filler stitch. The stitch pattern can also be elongated by adding two additional rows for a total of seven non-cabling rows between cabling rows.

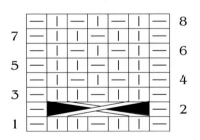

Panel of 7 sts

Row 1 and all other WS rows: (K1, p2) twice, k1
Row 2: P1, 1/3/1 RC, p1
Rows 4, 6 and 8: (P1, k1) three times, p1

2/1/2 Knit Crosses

1. Slip the next three stitches to a cable needle and hold at the back of the work.

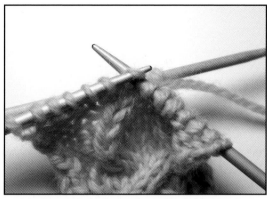

2. Knit the next two stitches from the left-hand needle.

3. Slip the left-most stitch from the cable needle back to the left-hand needle and knit it.

4. Knit the two stitches from the cable needle.

2/1/2 Right Cross

2/1/2 Left Cross

1. Slip the next three stitches to a cable needle and hold at the front of the work.

2. Knit the next two stitches from the left-hand needle.

3. Slip the left-most stitch from the cable needle back to the left-hand needle and knit it.

4. Knit the two stitches from the cable needle.

Pattern 5.10: Use this stitch pattern as an alternative to the traditional Aran Honeycomb (pattern 4.8).

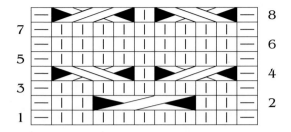

Panel of 11 sts

Row 1 and all other WS rows: K1, p9, k1
Row 2: P1, k2, 2/1/2 RC, k2, p1
Row 4: P1, 2/2 RC, k1, 2/2 LC, p1
Row 6: P1, k9, p1
Row 8: P1, 2/2 LC, k1, 2/2 RC, p1

Ideas for Further Exploration

1. Elongate this pattern by adding two (or four) non-cabling rows between rows 5 and 8.

2. Fill the center of this pattern with garter stitch.

2/1/2 Purl Crosses

2/1/2 Right Purl Cross

1. Slip the next three stitches to a cable needle and hold at the back of the work.

2. Knit the next two stitches from the left-hand needle.

3. Slip the left-most stitch from the cable needle back to the left-hand needle, then bring the cable needle to the front of and to the left of that stitch.

4. Purl the stitch from the left-hand needle.

5. Knit the two stitches from the cable needle.

1. Slip the next two stitches to a cable needle and hold at the front of the work. Slip the next stitch to a cable needle and hold at the back of the work.

2. Knit the next two stitches from the left-hand needle.

2/1/2 Left Purl Cross

3. Purl the stitch from the back cable needle.

4. Knit the two stitches from the front cable needle.

Pattern 5.11: This stitch pattern—often called the Five-Fold Aran Braid—illustrates what happens when a braid panel is opened up laterally by the addition of a single purl stitch between each pair of knit ribs.

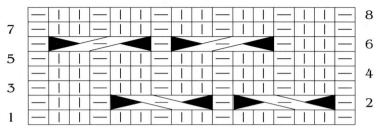

Panel of 16 sts

Row 1 and all other WS rows: (K1, p2) five times, k1
Row 2: (P1, 2/1/2 LPC) twice, p1, k2, p1
Rows 4 and 8: (P1, k2) five times, p1
Row 6: P1, k2, (p1, 2/1/2 RPC) twice, p1

Ideas for Further Exploration

1. Make an even looser version of this braid by stretching the stitch pattern vertically—add two (or four) additional non-cabling rows between the cabling rows.

2. This stitch pattern is almost always seen in the panel version of 16 stitches. How could the panel be widened?

Pattern 5.12: This is great example of a situation where a five-stitch cross is preferable to a four-stitch cross, because the twisted rib used as a filler stitch is based on an odd number of stitches. The 2/1/2 cross used here is a bit more refined than the 2/3 cross used in pattern 5.2.

Panel of 15 sts

Row 1 (WS): K5, p2, k1, p2, k4
Row 2: P5, 2/1/2 LPC, p5
Row 3: K5, p2, k1, p2, k5
Row 4: P4, 2/1 RC, p1, 2/1 LC, p4
Row 5: K4, p3, k1, p3, k4
Row 6: P3, 2/1 RPC, k1tbl, p1, k1tbl, 2/1 LPC, p3
Row 7: K3, p2, (k1, p1) twice, k1, p2, k3
Row 8: P2, 2/1 RC, (p1, k1tbl) twice, p1, 2/1 LC, p2
Row 9: K2, p3, (k1, p1) three times, p2, k2
Row 10: P1, 2/1 RPC, (k1tbl, p1) three times, k1tbl, 2/1 LPC, p1
Row 11: K1, p2, (k1, p1) four times, k1, p2, k1
Row 12: P1, k2, (p1, k1tbl) four times, p1, k2, p1
Row 13: K1, p2, (k1, p1) four times, k1, p2, k1
Row 14: P1, 2/1 LPC, (k1tbl, p1) three times, k1tbl, 2/1 RPC, p1
Row 15: K2, p3, (k1, p1) three times, p2, k2
Row 16: P2, 2/1 LPC, (p1, k1tbl) twice, p1, 2/1 RPC, p2
Row 17: K3, p2, (k1, p1) twice, k1, p2, k3
Row 18: P3, 2/1 LPC, k1tbl, p1, k1tbl, 2/1 RPC, p3
Row 19: K4, p3, k1, p3, k4
Row 20: P4, 2/1 LPC, p1, 2/1 RPC, p4

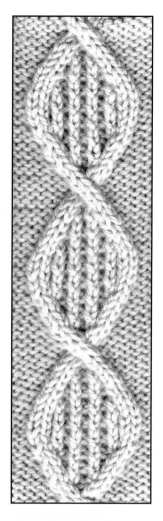

4/1 Knit Crosses

4/1 Right Cross

1. Slip the next stitch to a cable needle and hold at the back of the work.

2. Knit the next four stitches from the left-hand needle.

3. Knit the stitch from the cable needle.

4/1 Left Cross

1. Slip the next four stitches to a cable needle and hold at the front of the work.

2. Knit the next stitch from the left-hand needle.

3. Knit the four stitches from the cable needle.

4/1 Purl Crosses

4/1 Right Purl Cross

1. Slip the next stitch to a cable needle and hold at the back of the work.

2. Knit the next four stitches from the left-hand needle.

3. Purl the stitch from the cable needle.

4/1 Left Purl Cross

1. Slip the next four stitches to a cable needle and hold at the front of the work.

2. Purl the next stitch from the left-hand needle.

3. Knit the four stitches from the cable needle.

Pattern 5.13: This is a big, bold cable with four-stitch knit ribs. Note that the outer background is knitted instead of purled.

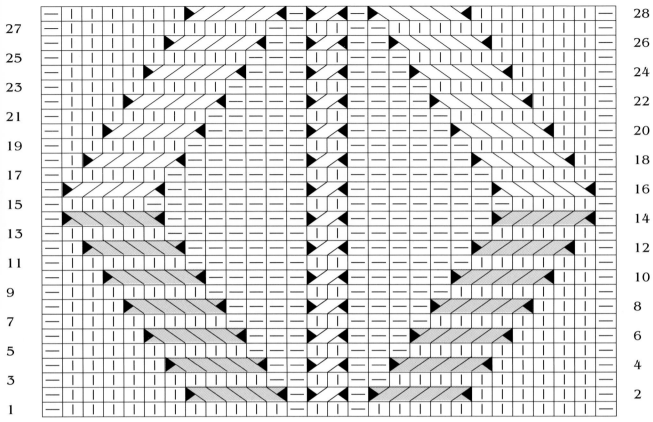

Panel of 28 stitches

Row 1 (WS): K1, p11, k1, p2, k1, p11, k1
Row 2: P1, k6, 4/1 RPC, p1, 1/1 RC, p1, 4/1 LPC, k6, p1
Rows 3 and 27: K1, p10, k2, p2, k2, p10, k1
Row 4: P1, k5, 4/1 RPC, p2, 1/1 RC, p2, 4/1 LPC, k5, p1
Rows 5 and 25: K1, p9, k3, p2, k3, p9, k1
Row 6: P1, k4, 4/1 RPC, p3, 1/1 RC, p3, 4/1 LPC, k4, p1
Rows 7 and 23: K1, p8, k4, p2, k4, p8, k1
Row 8: P1, k3, 4/1 RPC, p4, 1/1 RC, p4, 4/1 LPC, k3, p1
Rows 9 and 21: K1, p7, k5, p2, k5, p7, k1

Row 10: P1, k2, 4/1 RPC, p5, 1/1 RC, p5, 4/1 LPC, k2, p1
Rows 11 and 19: K1, p6, k6, p2, k6, p6, k1
Row 12: P1, k1, 4/1 RPC, p6, 1/1 RC, p6, 4/1 LPC, k1, p1
Rows 13 and 17: K1, p5, k7, p2, k7, p5, k1
Row 14: P1, 4/1 RPC, p7, 1/1 RC, p7, 4/1 LPC, p1
Row 15: K1, p4, k8, p2, k8, p4, k1
Row 16: P1, 4/1 LC, p7, 1/1 RC, p7, 4/1 RC, p1
Row 18: P1, k1, 4/1 LC, p6, 1/1 RC, p6, 4/1 RC, k1, p1
Row 20: P1, k2, 4/1 LC, p5, 1/1 RC, p5, 4/1 RC, k2, p1
Row 22: P1, k3, 4/1 LC, p4, 1/1 RC, p4, 4/1 RC, k3, p1
Row 24: P1, k4, 4/1 LC, p3, 1/1 RC, p3, 4/1 RC, k4, p1
Row 26: P1, k5, 4/1 LC, p2, 1/1 RC, p2, 4/1 RC, k5, p1
Row 28: P1, k6, 4/1 LC, p1, 1/1 RC, p1, 4/1 RC, k6, p1

Chapter 6

Six-Stitch Crosses

When you think of six-stitch crosses, you likely think of 3/3 right and left knit crosses, or 3/3 right and left purl crosses. It's true: they are essential elements in a number of familiar cable stitch patterns. However, this group also includes some not-so-familiar members: stitch patterns where two stitches cross over four and stitch patterns where two groups of two outside stitches cross over two stationary central stitches. Pay close attention to the interesting dance steps you'll see in these cable stitch patterns.

You'll note that many of the four-stitch cable patterns in Chapter 4 have six-stitch counterparts in Chapter 6, a characteristic which becomes important to the discussion on designing original stitch patterns in Chapter 10.

2/4 Knit Crosses

2/4 Right Cross

1. Slip the next four stitches to a cable needle and hold at back of the work.

2. Knit the next two stitches from the left-hand needle.

3. Knit the four stitches from the cable needle.

2/4 Left Cross

1. Slip the next two stitches to a cable needle and hold at the front of the work.

2. Knit the next four stitches from the left-hand needle.

3. Knit the two stitches from the cable needle.

Pattern 6.1: This is a wide vertical rope pattern which makes a good alternative to the traditional rope.

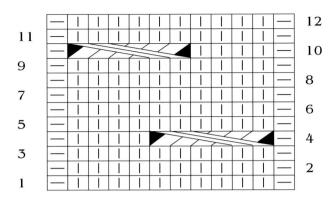

Panel of 12 stitches

Row 1 and all other WS rows: K1, p10, k1
Rows 2, 6, 8 and 12: P1, k10, p1
Row 4: P1, 2/4 LC, k4, p1
Row 10: P1, k4, 2/4 RC, p1

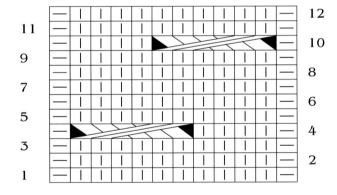

Panel of 12 stitches

Row 1 and all other WS rows: K1, p10, k1
Rows 2, 6, 8 and 12: P1, k10, p1
Row 4: P1, k4, 2/4 RC, p1
Row 10: P1, 2/4 RC, k4, p1

Pattern 6.2: Dazzle and amaze your knitting friends by using 2/4 knit crosses to "move" cables across the background. It appears that the cable is traveling to the right and left at the same time it is being crossed.

Note that this pattern includes all-knit crosses with stitches that change from knits to purls on the succeeding row. If you prefer, incorporate the purl stitches into the cross itself (refer to the chart to see which stitches of the cross should be purled instead of knitted). You will see this in several other stitch patterns in this chapter.

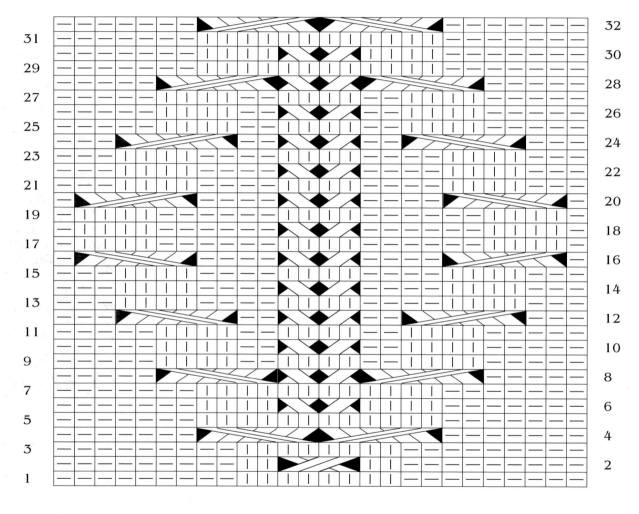

Panel of 26 stitches

Rows 1 and 3 (WS): K9, p8, k9
Row 2: P9, k2, 2/2 RC, k2, p9
Row 4: P7, 2/4 RC, 2/4 LC, p7
Rows 5, 7, 29 and 31: K7, p12, k7
Rows 6 and 30: P7, k4, 1/1 RC, 1/1 LC, k4, p7
Row 8: P5, 2/4 RC, 1/1 RC, 1/1 LC, 2/4 LC, p5
Rows 9, 11, 25 and 27: K5, (p4, k2) twice, p4, k5
Rows 10 and 26: P5, k4, p2, 1/1 RC, 1/1 LC, p2, k4, p5
Row 12: P3, 2/4 RC, p2, 1/1 RC, 1/1 LC, p2, 2/4 LC, p3
Rows 13, 15, 21 and 23: K3, (p4, k4) twice, p4, k3
Rows 14 and 22: P3, k4, p4, 1/1 RC, 1/1 LC, p4, k4, p3
Row 16: P1, 2/4 RC, p4, 1/1 RC, 1/1 LC, p4, 2/4 LC, p1
Rows 17 and 19: K1, (p4, k6) twice, p4, k1
Row 18: P1, k4, p6, 1/1 RC, 1/1 LC, p6, k4, p1
Row 20: P1, 2/4 LC, p4, 1/1 RC, 1/1 LC, p4, 2/4 RC, p1
Row 24: P3, 2/4 LC, p2, 1/1 RC, 1/1 LC, p2, 2/4 RC, p3
Row 28: P5, 2/4 LC, 1/1 RC, 1/1 LC, 2/4 RC, p5
Row 32: P7, 2/4 LC, 2/4 RC, p7

Ideas for Further Exploration

The technique of crossing and moving cables across background stitches simultaneously can be applied to other situations. What other cable patterns using these kinds of traveling lines can you create?

2/4 Purl Crosses

2/4 Right Purl Cross

1. Slip the next four stitches to a cable needle and hold at the back of the work.

2. Knit the next two stitches from the left-hand needle.

3. Purl the four stitches from the cable needle.

2/4 Left Purl Cross

1. Slip the next two stitches to a cable needle and hold at the front of the work.

2. Purl the next four stitches from the left-hand needle.

3. Knit the two stitches from the cable needle.

Pattern 6.3: Here is an excellent application of 2/4 purl crosses. The center plait spins out into two two-stitch knit ribs for eleven rows, which then flow back into the plait pattern once more.

Row 16 includes a 2/4 left cross (all stitches knit). As with the previous pattern, some of the stitches in that cross change from knits to purls on row 17. Again, if you prefer, incorporate the purl stitches into the cross as you work it.

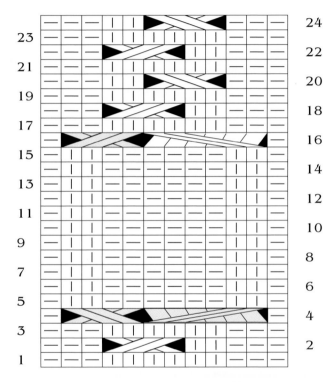

Panel of 12 stitches

Row 1 (WS): K3, p6, k3
Row 2: P3, k2, 2/2 RC, p3
Row 3: K3, p6, k3
Row 4: P1, 2/4 RPC, 2/2 LPC, p1
Rows 5, 7, 9, 11, 13 and 15: K1, p2, k6, p2, k1
Rows 6, 8, 10, 12 and 14: P1, k2, p6, k2, p1
Row 16: P1, 2/4 LC, 2/2 RPC, p1
Rows 17, 19, 21 and 23: K3, p6, k3
Rows 18 and 22: P3, k2, 2/2 RC, p3
Rows 20 and 24: P3, 2/2 LC, k2, p3

Ideas for Further Exploration

1. Instead of having the two-stitch ribs move out and then back in an oval shape, have them move in a diamond shape.

2. Repeat this pattern across a width of fabric. Have the two-stitch ribs move out, meet and cross, and move back in.

3/3 Knit Crosses

3/3 Right Cross

1. Slip the next three stitches to a cable needle and hold at the back of the work.

2. Knit the next three stitches from the left-hand needle.

3. Knit the three stitches from the cable needle.

3/3 Left Cross

1. Slip the next three stitches to a cable needle and hold at the front of the work.

2. Knit the next three stitches from the left-hand needle.

3. Knit the three stitches from the cable needle.

Pattern 6.4: Like their four-stitch counterparts, groups of six stitches form rope cables; the difference is that here there are five non-cabling rows between crosses instead of three. The same kinds of variations are possible with this rope cable as with the four-stitch rope cable.

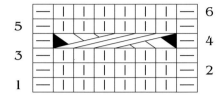

Panel of 8 stitches

Row 1 and all other WS rows: K1, p6, k1
Rows 2 and 6: P1, k6, p1
Row 4: P1, 3/3 RC, p1

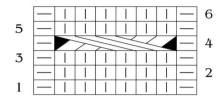

Panel of 8 stitches

Row 1 and all other WS rows: K1, p6, k1
Rows 2 and 6: P1, k6, p1
Row 4: P1, 3/3 LC, p1

Pattern 6.5: Alternating the direction of the crosses forms a wave cable.

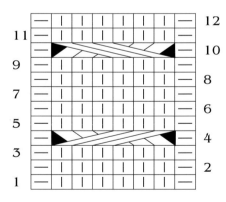

Panel of 8 stitches

Row 1 and all other WS rows: K1, p6, k1
Rows 2, 6, 8 and 12: P1, k6, p1
Row 4: P1, 3/3 RC, p1
Row 10: P1, 3/3 LC, p1

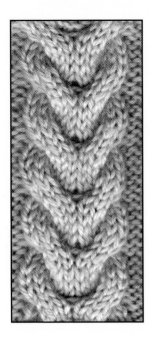

Pattern 6.6: Looking for a bolder horsehoe pattern? This fills the need perfectly.

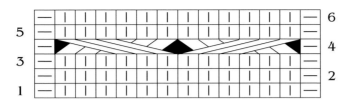

Panel of 14 stitches

Row 1 and all other WS rows: K1, p12, k1
Rows 2 and 6: P1, k12, p1
Row 4: P1, 3/3 RC, 3/3 LC, p1

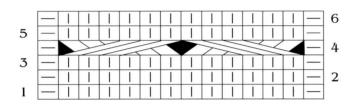

Panel of 14 stitches

Row 1 and all other WS rows: K1, p12, k1
Rows 2 and 6: P1, k12, p1
Row 4: P1, 3/3 LC, 3/3 RC, p1

Pattern 6.7: Adding or subtracting non-cabling rows to this plait will make it looser or tighter, depending on the effect you desire.

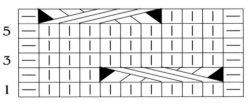

Panel of 11 stitches

Row 1 and all WS rows: K1, p9, k1
Row 2: P1, 3/3 LC, k3, p1
Row 4: P1, k9, p1
Row 6: P1, k3, 3/3 RC, p1

Pattern 6.8: Many bold knot patterns are possible using the 3/3 right and left crosses.

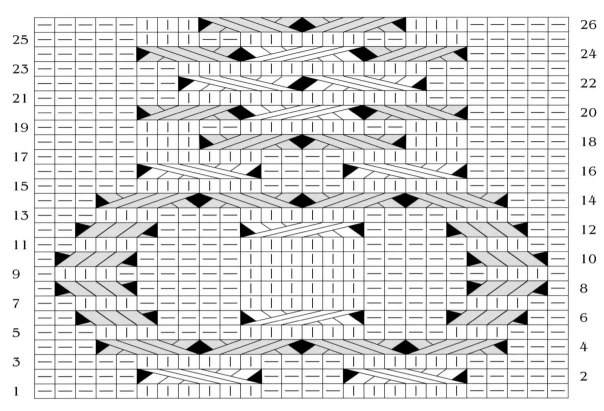

Panel of of 26 stitches

Rows 1 and 3 (WS): K5, p6, k4, p6, k5
Row 2: P5, 3/3 LC, p4, 3/3 LC, p5
Row 4: P3, (3/2 RPC, 3/2 LPC) twice, p3
Rows 5 and 13: K3, p3, k4, p6, k4, p3, k3
Row 6: P2, 3/1 RPC, p4, 3/3 RC, p4, 3/1 LPC, p2
Rows 7 and 11: K2, p3, k5, p6, k5, p3, k2
Row 8: P1, 3/1 RPC, p5, k6, p5, 3/1 LPC, p1
Row 9: K1, p3, k6, p6, k6, p3, k1
Row 10: P1, 3/1 LPC, p5, k6, p5, 3/1 RPC, p1
Row 12: P2, 3/1 LPC, p4, 3/3 RC, p4, 3/1 LPC, p2

Row 14: P3, (3/2 LPC, 3/2 RPC) twice, p3
Rows 15 and 17: K5, p6, k4, p6, k5
Row 16: P5, 3/3 LC, p4, 3/3 LC, p5
Row 18: P5, k3, 3/2 LPC, 3/2 RPC, k3, p5
Rows 19 and 25: K5, p3, k2, p6, k2, p3, k5
Row 20: P5, 3/2 LPC, 3/3 RC, 3/2 RPC, p5
Rows 21 and 23: K7, p12, k7
Row 22: P7, (3/3 LC) twice, p7
Row 24: P5, 3/2 RPC, 3/3 RC, 3/2 LPC, p5
Row 26: P5, k3, 3/2 RPC, 3/2 LPC, k3, p5

Pattern 6.9: This bold cable is lovely in this form, but also lends itself well to being filled with texture stitches such as moss and seed.

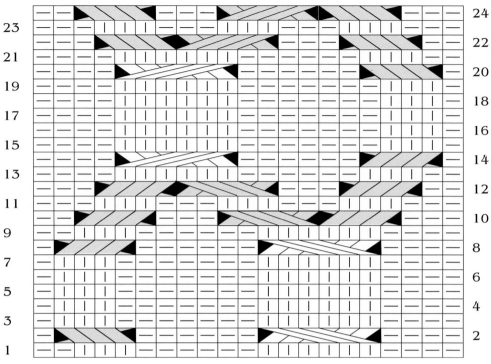

Panel of 21 stitches

Rows 1 and 9 (WS): K2, p3, k6, p6, k4
Row 2: P4, 3/3 LC, p6, 3/1 LPC, p1
Rows 3, 5 and 7: K1, p3, k7, p6, k4
Rows 4 and 6: P4, k6, p7, k3, p1
Row 8: P4, 3/3 LC, p6, 3/1 RPC, p1
Row 10: P3, 3/1 RPC, 3/2 LPC, p3, 3/1 RPC, p2
Rows 11 and 23: (K3, p3) three times, k3
Row 12: P2, 3/1 RPC, p3, 3/2 LPC, 3/1 RPC, p3

Rows 13 and 21: K4, p6, k6, p3, k2
Row 14: P1, 3/1 RPC, p6, 3/3 RC, p4
Rows 15, 17 and 19: K4, p6, k7, p3, k1
Rows 16 and 18: P1, k3, p7, k6, p4
Row 20: P1, 3/1 LPC, p6, 3/3 RC, p4
Row 22: P2, 3/1 LPC, p3, 3/2 RPC, 3/1 LPC, p3
Row 24: P3, 3/1 LPC, 3/2 RPC, p3, 3/1 LPC, p2

3/3 Purl Crosses

3/3 Right Purl Cross

1. Slip the next three stitches to a cable needle and hold at the back of the work.

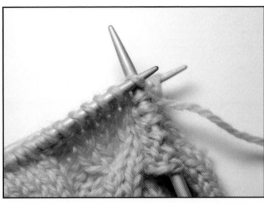

2. Knit the next three stitches from the left-hand needle.

3. Purl the three stitches from the cable needle.

3/3 Left Purl Cross

1. Slip the next three stitches to a cable needle and hold at the front of the work.

2. Purl the next three stitches from the left-hand needle.

3. Knit the three stitches from the cable needle.

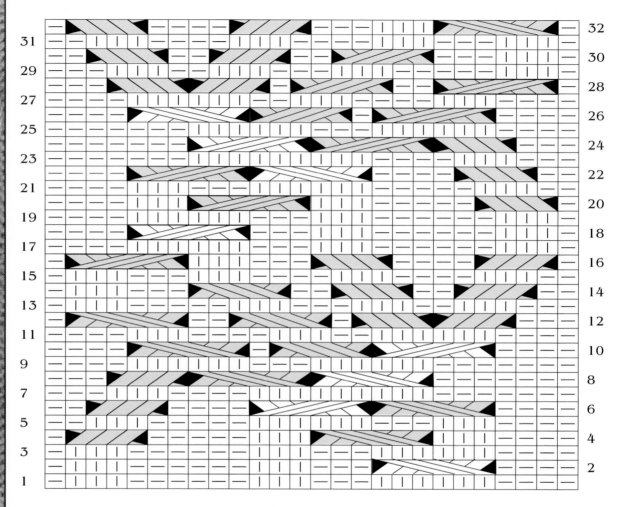

Pattern 6.10: Here is a freewheeling knot pattern which requires that the knitter pay close attention!

Panel of 26 stitches

Rows 1 and 3 (WS): K1, p3, k6, p3, k3, p6, k4
Row 2: P4, 3/3 LC, p3, k3, p6, k3, p1
Row 4: P4, k3, 3/3 LPC, k3, p5, 3/1 RPC, p1
Row 5: K2, p3, k5, p6, k3, p3, k4
Row 6: P4, 3/3 LPC, 3/3 RC, p4, 3/1 RPC, p2

Row 7: K3, p3, k4, p9, k7
Row 8: P7, 3/3 LC, 3/3 LPC, 3/1 RPC, p8
Row 9: K4, p6, k3, p6, k7
Row 10: P4, 3/3 RC, 3/2 LPC, p1, 3/3 LPC, p4
Row 11: (K4, p3) twice, k2, p6, k4
Row 12: P3, 3/1 RPC, 3/1 LPC, p1, 3/2 LPC, p2, 3/3 LPC, p1
Row 13: K1, p3, k5, p3, k3, p3, k2, p3, k3
Row 14: P2, 3/1 RPC, p2, 3/1 LPC, p2, 3/2 LPC, p3, k3, p1
Row 15: K1, p3, k3, (p3, k4) twice, p3, k2
Row 16: P1, 3/1 RPC, p4, 3/1 LPC, p3, k3, 3/3 RPC, p1
Row 17: K4, p6, k3, p3, k6, p3, k1
Row 18: P1, k3, p6, k3, p3, 3/3 RC, p4
Row 19: K4, p6, k3, p3, k6, p3, k1
Row 20: P1, 3/1 LPC, p5, k3, 3/3 RPC, k3, p4
Row 21: K4, p3, k3, p6, k5, p3, k2
Row 22: P2, 3/1 LPC, p4, 3/3 LC, 3/3 RPC, p4
Row 23: K7, p9, k4, p3, k3
Row 24: P3, 3/1 LPC, 3/3 RPC, 3/3 RC, p7
Row 25: K7, p6, k3, p6, k4
Row 26: P4, 3/3 RPC, p1, 3/2 RPC, 3/3 LC, p4
Row 27: K4, p6, k2, p3, k4, p3, k4
Row 28: P1, 3/3 RPC, p2, 3/2 RPC, p1, 3/1 RPC, 3/1 LPC, p3
Row 29: K3, p3, k2, p3, k3, p3, k5, p3, k1
Row 30: P1, k3, p3, 3/2 RPC, p2, 3/1 RPC, p2, 3/1 LPC, p2
Row 31: K2, p3, (k4, p3) twice, k3, p3, k1
Row 32: P1, 3/3 LPC, k3, p3, 3/1 RPC, p4, 3/1 LPC, p1

Ideas for Further Exploration

How many other knot patterns can you create using 3/3 crosses, both knit and purl?

Pattern 6.11: Wow, what a massive cable stitch pattern! If you're looking for drama, this is the stitch to use. It features both 3/3 knit crosses and 3/3 purl crosses.

Panel of 38 stitches

Rows 1, 3 and 41 (WS): K1, p3, k2, p3, k7, p6, k7, p3, k2, p3, k1
Rows 2 and 42: P1, k3, p2, k3, p7, k6, p7, k3, p2, k3, p1
Row 4: P1, 3/1 LPC, 3/1 RPC, p7, 3/3 LC, p7, 3/1 LPC, 3/1 RPC, p1
Rows 5 and 39: K2, p6, k8, p6, k8, p6, k2
Row 6: P2, 3/3 LC, p6, 3/2 RPC, 3/2 LPC, p6, 3/3 LC, p2
Rows 7 and 37: K2, p6, k6, p3, k4, p3, k6, p6, k2
Row 8: P2, k3, 3/1 LPC, p3, 3/2 RPC, p4, 3/2 LPC, p3, 3/1 RPC, k3, p2
Rows 9 and 35: K2, p3, k1, p3, k3, p3, k8, p3, k3, p3, k1, p3, k2
Row 10: P2, (3/1 LPC) twice, 3/2 RPC, p8, 3/2 LPC, (3/1 RPC) twice, p2
Rows 11 and 33: K3, p3, k1, p6, k12, p6, k1, p3, k3
Row 12: P3, 3/1 LPC, 3/3 RC, p12, 3/3 RC, 3/1 RPC, p3
Rows 13 and 31: K4, p9, k12, p9, k4
Row 14: P4, 3/3 LC, 3/3 LPC, p6, 3/3 RPC, 3/3 LC, p4
Rows 15 and 29: K4, p6, k3, p3, k6, p3, k3, p6, k4
Row 16: P3, 3/1 RPC, (3/3 LPC) twice, (3/3 RPC) twice, 3/1 LPC, p3
Rows 17 and 27: K3, p3, k4, p3, k3, p6, k3, p3, k4, p3, k3
Row 18: P2, 3/1 RPC, p4, 3/3 LPC, 3/3 LC, 3/3 RPC, p4, 3/1 LPC, p2
Rows 19 and 25: K2, p3, k8, p12, k8, p3, k2
Row 20: P1, 3/1 RPC, p8, (3/3 RC) twice, p8, 3/1 LPC, p1
Rows 21 and 23: K1, p3, k9, p12, k9, p3, k1
Row 22: P1, k3, p9, k3, 3/3 LC, k3, p9, k3, p1
Row 24: P1, 3/1 LPC, p8, (3/3 RC) twice, p8, 3/1 RPC, p1
Row 26: P2, 3/1 LPC, p4, 3/3 RPC, 3/3 LC, 3/3 LPC, p4, 3/1 LPC, p2
Row 28: P3, 3/1 LPC, (3/3 RPC) twice, (3/3 LPC) twice, 3/1 RPC, p3
Row 30: P4, 3/3 LC, 3/3 RPC, p6, 3/3 LPC, 3/3 LC, p4
Row 32: P3, 3/1 RPC, 3/3 RC, p12, 3/3 RC, 3/1 LPC, p3
Row 34: P2, (3/1 RPC) twice, 3/2 LPC, p8, 3/2 RPC, (3/1 LPC) twice, p2
Row 36: P2, k3, 3/1 RPC, p3, 3/2 LPC, p4, 3/2 RPC, p3, 3/1 LPC, k3, p2
Row 38: P2, 3/3 LC, p6, 3/2 LPC, 3/2 RPC, p6, 3/3 LC, p2
Row 40: P1, 3/1 RPC, 3/1 LPC, p7, 3/3 LC, p7, 3/1 RPC, 3/1 LPC, p1

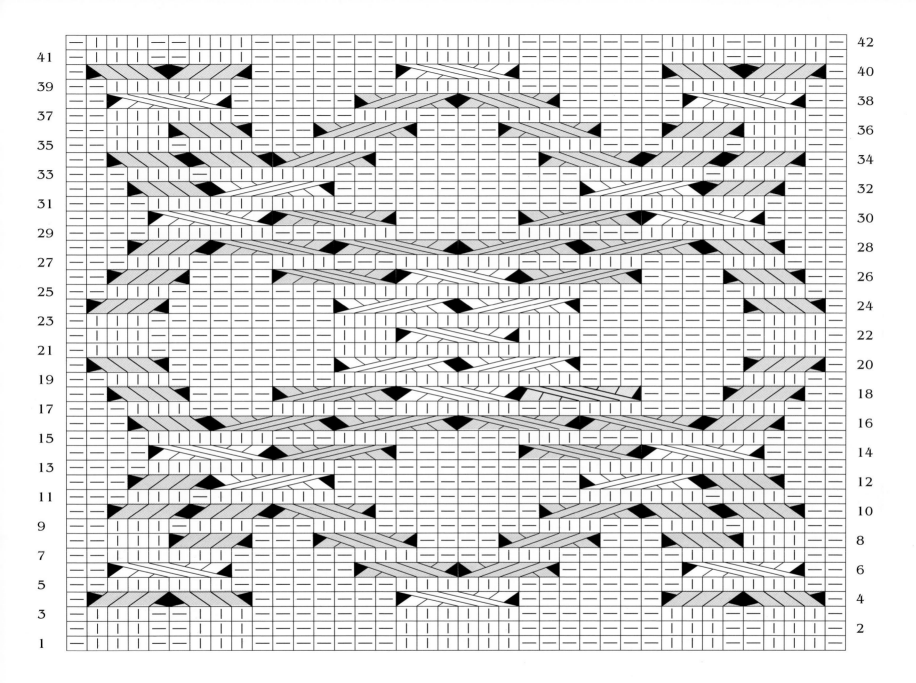

2/2/2 Knit Crosses: In this group of crosses, two groups of two outer stitches exchange places, leaving the center two stitches in place. All stitches are knitted.

2/2/2 Right Cross

1. Slip the next four stitches to a cable needle and hold at the back of the work.

2. Knit the next two stitches from the left-hand needle.

3. Slip the two left-most stitches from the cable needle back to the left-hand needle, then bring the cable needle to the front of and to the left of those two stitches.

4. Knit the two stitches from the left-hand needle.

4. Knit the two stitches from the cable needle.

1. Slip the next two stitches to a cable needle and hold at the front of the work, then slip the following two stitches to second cable needle and hold at the back of the work.

2. Knit the next two stitches from the left-hand needle.

2/2/2 Left Cross

3. Knit the two stitches from the back cable needle.

4. Knit the two stitches from the front cable needle.

2/2/2 Reverse Crosses: The center two stitches in this group are in front of the two sets of outer stitches as they exchange places.

2/2/2 Right Reverse Cross

1. Slip the next two stitches to a cable needle and hold at the back of the work, then slip the following two stitches to a second cable needle and hold at the front of the work.

2. Knit the next two stitches from the left-hand needle.

3. Knit the two stitches from the front cable needle.

4. Knit the two stitches from the back cable needle.

1. Slip the next four stitches to a cable needle and hold at the front of the work.

2. Knit the next two stitches from the left-hand needle.

2/2/2 Left Reverse Cross

3. Slip the two left-most stitches from the cable needle back to the left-hand needle, then pass the cable needle to the back of the work. Knit the two stitches from the left-hand needle.

4. Knit the two stitches from the cable needle at the back.

Pattern 6.12: This and the following patterns illustrate very well the use of 2/2/2 knit and 2/2/2 reverse crosses. Note the combinations and how they affect the appearance of the cable: in patterns 6.12 and 6.13, both crosses are in the same direction, either left or right. In patterns 6.14 and 6.15, the crosses are in opposite directions.

All four of these patterns may also be worked in nine-stitch versions, with three groups of three-stitch ribs.

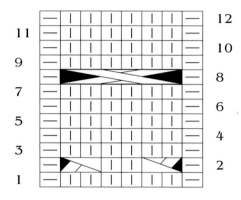

Panel of 8 stitches

Row 1 and all other WS rows: K1, p6, k1
Row 2: P1, 2/2/2 LRC, p1
Rows 4, 6, 10 and 12: P1, k6, p1
Row 8: P1, 2/2/2 LC, p1

Pattern 6.13

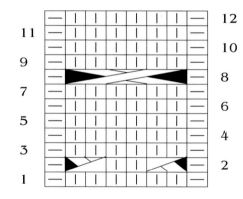

Panel of 8 stitches

Row 1 and all other WS rows: K1, p6, k1
Row 2: P1, 2/2/2 RRC, p1
Rows 4, 6, 10 and 12: P1, k6, p1
Row 8: P1, 2/2/2 RC, p1

Pattern 6.14

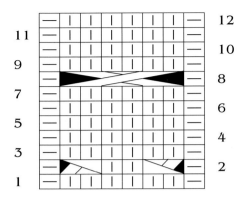

Panel of 8 stitches

Row 1 and all other WS rows: K1, p6, k1
Row 2: P1, 2/2/2 LRC, p1
Rows 4, 6, 10 and 12: P1, k6, p1
Row 8: P1, 2/2/2 RC, p1

Pattern 6.15

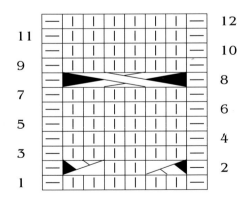

Panel of 8 stitches

Row 1 and all other WS rows: K1, p6, k1
Row 2: P1, 2/2/2 RRC, p1
Rows 4, 6, 10 and 12: P1, k6, p1
Row 8: P1, 2/2/2 LC, p1

Pattern 6.16: This is one of my very favorite stitch patterns. I've always been intrigued by the way the knit ribs wrap themselves around each other. Note that the crosses on rows 2, 10, 14 and 22 may be worked according to the instructions given in the key (that is, as all-knit crosses), with some of the stitches in those crosses changing to purls on the rows 3, 11, 15 and 23. Alternatively, incorporate the purl stitches into the crosses and avoid having to change them on the wrong-side rows.

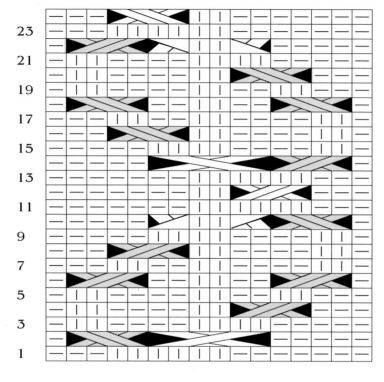

Panel of 16 stitches

Row 1 (WS): K3, p6, k7
Row 2: P5, 2/2/2 RC, 2/2 LPC, p1
Row 3: K1, p2, k4, p4, k5
Row 4: P3, 2/2 RPC, k2, p4, k2, p1
Row 5: K1, p2, k4, p2, k2, p2, k3
Row 6: P1, 2/2 RPC, p2, k2, p2, 2/2 RPC, p1
Row 7: K3, p2, k2, p2, k4, p2, k1
Row 8: P1, k2, p4, k2, 2/2 RPC, p3
Row 9: K5, p4, k4, p2, k1
Row 10: P1, 2/2 LPC, 2/2/2 RRC, p5
Row 11: K7, p6, k3
Row 12: P3, 2/2 RC, k2, p7
Row 13: K7, p6, k3
Row 14: P1, 2/2 RPC, 2/2/2 LC, p5
Row 15: K5, p4, k4, p2, k1
Row 16: P1, k2, p4, k2, 2/2 LPC, p3
Row 17: K3, p2, k2, p2, k4, p2, k1
Row 18: P1, 2/2 LPC, p2, k2, p2, 2/2 LPC, p1
Row 19: K1, p2, k4, p2, k2, p2, k3
Row 20: P3, 2/2 LPC, k2, p4, k2, p1
Row 21: K1, p2, k4, p4, k5
Row 22: P5, 2/2/2 LRC, 2/2 RPC, p1
Row 23: K3, p6, k7
Row 24: P7, k2, 2/2 LC, p3

2/2/2 Purl Crosses:

Here, two groups of two outer stitches exchange places, leaving the center two stitches in place. The outer stitches are knitted; the center two stitches are purled.

1. Slip the next four stitches to a cable needle and hold at the back of the work.

2. Knit the next two stitches from the left-hand needle.

2/2/2 Right Purl Cross

3. Slip the two left-most stitches from the cable needle back to the left-hand needle, then bring the cable needle to the front of and to the left of those two stitches.

4. Purl the two stitches from the left-hand needle.

5. Knit the two stitches from the cable needle.

2/2/2 Left Purl Cross

1. *Slip the next two stitches to a cable needle and hold at the front of the work. Slip the following two stitches to a cable needle and hold at the back of the work.*

2. *Knit the next two stitches from the left-hand needle.*

3. *Purl the two stitches from the back cable needle.*

4. *Knit the two stitches from the front cable needle.*

Pattern 6.17: This simple chain pattern can be used as another alternative to the basic four-stitch rope pattern.

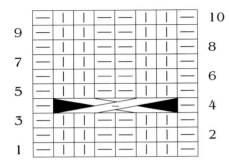

Panel of 8 stitches

Row 1 and all other WS rows: K1, p2, k2, p2, k1
Rows 2, 6, 8 and 10: P1, k2, p2, k2, p1
Row 4: P1, 2/2/2 RPC, p1

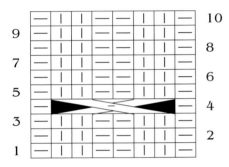

Panel of 8 stitches

Row 1 and all other WS rows: K1, p2, k2, p2, k1
Rows 2, 6, 8 and 10: P1, k2, p2, k2, p1
Row 4: P1, 2/2/2 LPC, p1

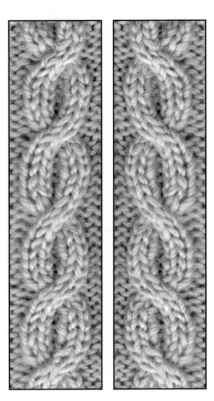

Ideas for Further Exploration

Set up a basic k2, p2 ribbing and work for approximately one inch. Begin working a series of these crosses over that ribbing (you may space the crosses closer together if desired). Alternate crossing each group of two stitches with its neighbors to form a trellis pattern. Finish with another section of plain k2, p2 ribbing.

Seven-Stitch Crosses

This is the shortest chapter in the book, and yet I find it one of the most interesting. I really think the crosses featured here are underused—this destination is one of the hidden gems of the Land of Cables because these crosses are so versatile. Here, they are featured in patterns with lace, with filler stitches, and with ribbings. Take some time to study them. They may inspire you to create even more interesting additions to this group!

3/4 Knit Crosses

3/4 Right Knit Cross

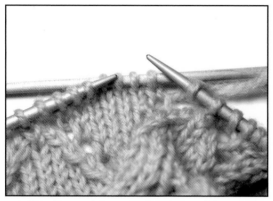

1. Slip the next four stitches to a cable needle and hold at the back of the work.

2. Knit the next three stitches from the left-hand needle.

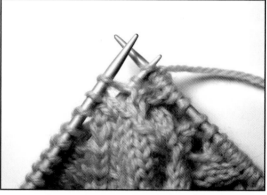

3. Knit the four stitches from the cable needle.

3/4 Left Knit Cross

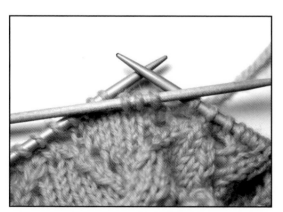

1. Slip the next three stitches to a cable needle and hold at the front of the work.

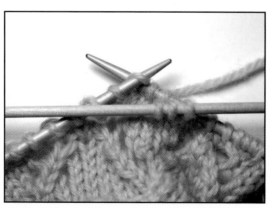

2. Knit the next four stitches from the left-hand needle.

3. Knit the three stitches from the cable needle.

Pattern 7.1: You almost have to look twice to find the 3/4 crosses in this cable pattern. They blend into the lace pattern, and yet are integral to the overall appearance.

Multiple of 10 stitches + 13

Row 1 and all other WS rows: K1, purl to last stitch, k1
Row 2: P1, k5, yo, SSK, k4, *k4, yo, SSK, k4; rep from *, end p1
Row 4: P1, k3, k2tog, yo, k1, yo, SSK, k3, *k2, k2tog, yo, k1, yo, SSK, k3; rep from *, end p1
Row 6: P1, k2, k2tog, yo, k3, yo, SSK, k2, *k1, k2tog, yo, k3, yo, SSK, k2; rep from *, end p1
Row 8: P1, k1, k2tog, yo, k5, yo, SSK, k1, *k2tog, yo, k5, yo, SSK, k1; rep from *, end p1
Row 10: P1, k2tog, yo, k7, *yo, sl2—k1—psso, yo, k7; rep from *, end yo, SSK, p1
Row 12: P1, k2, 3/4 RC, *k3, 3/4 RC; rep from *, end k2, p1

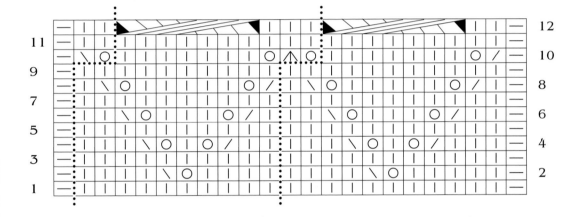

3/1/3 Knit Crosses

3/1/3 Right Cross

1. Slip the next four stitches to a cable needle and hold at the back of the work.

2. Knit the next three stitches from the left-hand needle.

3. Slip the left-most stitch from the cable needle back to the left-hand needle and knit it.

4. Knit the three stitches from the cable needle.

3/1/3 Left Cross

1. Slip the next four stitches to a cable needle and hold at the front of the work.

2. Knit the next three stitches from the left-hand needle.

3. Slip the left-most stitch from the cable needle back to the left-hand needle and knit it.

4. Knit the three stitches from the cable needle.

Pattern 7.2: Need a dramatic center panel for your next Aran sweater? Try this one. The three-stitch cable ribs form a large diamond—in this version, filled with moss stitch.

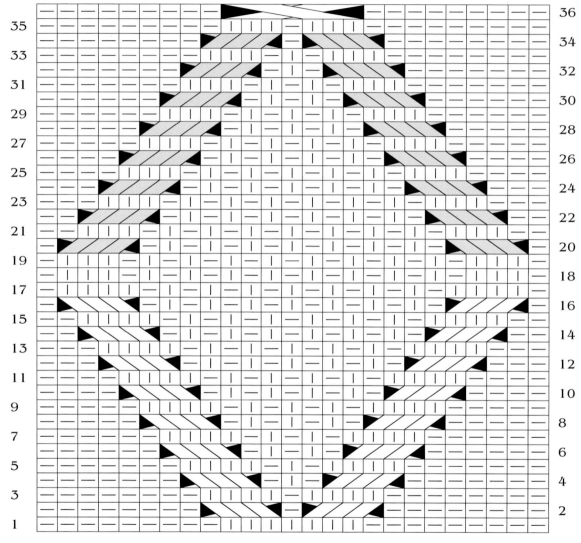

Panel of 25 stitches

Row 1: K9, p7, k9
Row 2: P8, 3/1 RC, p1, 3/1 LC, p8
Row 3 and all remaining WS rows: Knit the knits and purl the purls
Row 4: P7, 3/1 RC, p1, k1, p1, 3/1 LC, p7
Row 6: P6, 3/1 RC, (p1, k1) twice, p1, 3/1 LC, p6
Row 8: P5, 3/1 RC, (p1, k1) three times, p1, 3/1 LC, p5
Row 10: P4, 3/1 RC, (p1, k1) four times, p1, 3/1 LC, p4
Row 12: P3, 3/1 RC, (p1, k1) five times, p1, 3/1 LC, p3
Row 14: P2, 3/1 RC, (p1, k1) six times, p1, 3/1 LC, p2
Row 16: P1, 3/1 RC, (p1, k1) seven times, p1, 3/1 LC, p1
Row 18: P1, k3, (p1, k1) eight times, p1, k3, p1
Row 20: P1, 3/1 LPC, (p1, k1) seven times, p1, 3/1 RPC, p1
Row 22: P2, 3/1 LPC, (p1, k1) six times, p1, 3/1 RPC, p2
Row 24: P3, 3/1 LPC, (p1, k1) five times, p1, 3/1 RPC, p3
Row 26: P4, 3/1 LPC, (p1, k1) four times, p1, 3/1 RPC, p4
Row 28: P5, 3/1 LPC, (p1, k1) three times, p1, 3/1 RPC, p5
Row 30: P6, 3/1 LPC, (p1, k1) twice, p1, 3/1 RPC, p6
Row 32: P7, 3/1 LPC, p1, k1, p1, 3/1 RPC, p7
Row 34: P8, 3/1 LPC, p1, 3/1 RPC, p8
Row 36: P9, 3/1/3 LPC, p9

Ideas for Further Exploration

1. Make the diamond bigger or smaller by adding or subtracting 3/1 crossing rows.

2. For a very wide and dramatic panel, place three of these diamonds together in half-drop formation (the center diamond nested between the two outer ones).

3. Repeat the 3/1/3 cross once every six rows two, or even three, times.

3/1/3 Purl Crosses

3/1/3 Right Purl Cross

1. Slip the next four stitches to a cable needle and hold at the back of the work.

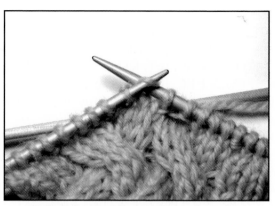

2. Knit the next three stitches from the left-hand needle.

3. Slip the left-most stitch from the cable needle back to the left-hand needle and purl it.

4. Knit the three stitches from the cable needle.

1. Slip the next four stitches to a cable needle and hold at the front of the work.

2. Knit the next three stitches from the left-hand needle.

3. Slip the left-most stitch from the cable needle back to the left-hand needle and purl it.

4. Knit the three stitches from the cable needle.

3/1/3 Left Purl Cross

Pattern 7.3: This wonderfully bold cable features a central braid pattern based on 3/1/3 right and left purl crosses. That center braid can be used as the basis for a number of variations in which the three-stitch ribs travel outward before coming back to meet and cross again.

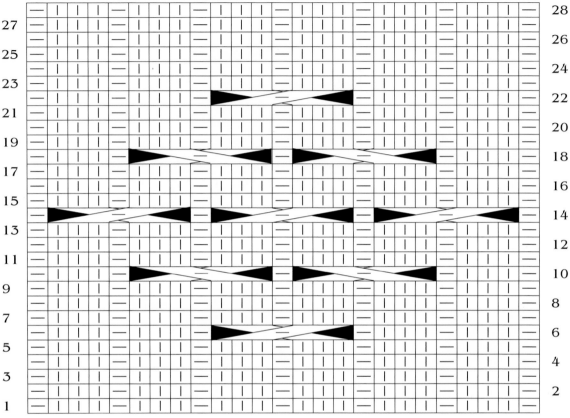

Panel of 25 stitches

Row 1 and all other WS rows: (K1, p3) six times, k1
Rows 2, 4, 8, 12, 16, 20, 24, 26 and 28: (P1, k3) six times, p1
Rows 6 and 22: (P1, k3) twice, p1, 3/1/3 RPC, (p1, k3) twice, p1
Rows 10 and 18: P1, k3, p1, 3/1/3 LPC, p1, 3/1/3 LPC, p1, k3, p1
Row 14: (P1, 3/1/3 RPC) three times, p1

Eight-Stitch Crosses and Beyond

These are the heavyweights of the cable world—big, dramatic cables which command an audience. Use them judiciously in your designs, as they can overwhelm smaller, more delicate cables. Make them the focal point of a piece, though, and you will be richly rewarded.

Note that cable splay can be a significant problem with this group. Plan for increases at the bottom and decreases at the top of each cable. Loosen your tension slightly when crossing the cable. Above all, enjoy them!

Chapter 8—Eight-Stitch Crosses

189

4/4 Knit Crosses

4/4 Right Cross

1. Slip the next four stitches to a cable needle and hold at the back of the work.

2. Knit the next four stitches from the left-hand needle.

3. Knit the four stitches from the cable needle.

4/4 Left Cross

1. Slip the next four stitches to a cable needle and hold at the front of the work.

2. Knit the next four stitches from the left-hand needle.

3. Knit the four stitches from the cable needle.

Pattern 8.1: This is a basic rope cable, worked over eight stitches. It pairs nicely with other bold, bulky cable stitch patterns.

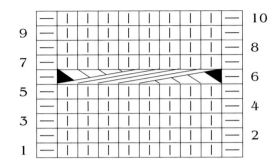

Panel of 10 stitches

Row 1 and all other WS rows: K1, p8, k1
Rows 2, 4, 8 and 10: P1, k8, p1
Row 6: P1, 4/4 RC, p1

Pattern 8.2: Alternate the direction of the crosses in pattern 8.1 and form a wave cable instead of a rope cable. Note that instead of nine non-cabling rows between crosses as in pattern 8.1, there are seven.

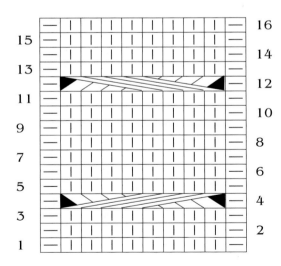

Panel of 10 stitches

Row 1 and all other WS rows: K1, p8, k1
Rows 2, 6, 8, 10, 14 and 16: P1, k8, p1
Row 4: P1, 4/4 RC, p1
Row 12: P1, 4/4 LC, p1

Pattern 8.3: Note that this cable stitch pattern features 4/4 crosses on rows 4, 10, 14, and 20. Three non-cabling rows (rows 11-13) separate the two 4/4 crosses on rows 10 and 14, while five non-cabling rows rows (21, 22, and 1-3) separate the 4/4 crosses on rows 20 and 4. It's a subtle distinction, but if you look carefully at the swatch, you can see that the crosses on rows 10 and 14 are slightly tighter than the ones on rows 20 and 4.

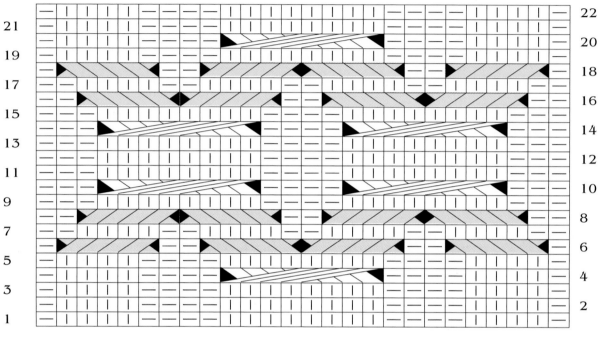

Panel of 26 stitches

Rows 1, 3, 5, 19 and 21 (WS): K1, p4, k4, p8, k4, p4, k1
Rows 2 and 22: P1, k4, p4, k8, p4, k4, p1
Rows 4 and 20: P1, k4, p4, 4/4 RC, p4, k4, p1
Row 6: P1, (4/1 LPC, p2, 4/1 RPC) twice, p1
Rows 7 and 17: (K2, p4) four times, k2
Row 8: (P2, 4/1 LPC, 4/1 RPC) twice, p2
Rows 9, 11, 13 and 15: K3, p8, k4, p8, k3
Rows 10 and 14: P3, 4/4 RC, p4, 4/4 RC, p3
Row 12: P3, k8, p4, k8, p3
Row 16: (P2, 4/1 RPC, 4/1 LPC) twice, p2
Row 18: P1, (4/1 RPC, p2, 4/1 LPC) twice, p1

5/4 Knit Crosses

5/4 Right Cross

1. Slip the next four stitches to a cable needle and hold at the back of the work.

2. Knit the next five stitches from the left-hand needle.

3. Knit the four stitches from the cable needle.

5/4 Left Cross

1. Slip the next five stitches to a cable needle and hold at the front of the work.

2. Knit the next four stitches from the left-hand needle.

3. Knit the five stitches from the cable needle.

Pattern 8.4: This is another example of an "uneven" cable, in which a larger number of stitches crosses over a smaller number of stitches. In this case, five stitches cross over four. Eleven non-cabling rows separate each cross. It's a bold, but not tight, cable.

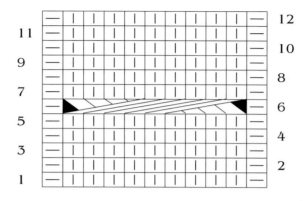

Panel of 11 stitches

Row 1 and all other WS rows: K1, p9, k1
Rows 2, 4, 8, 10 and 12: P1, k9, p1
Row 6: P1, 5/4 RC, p1

5/5 Knit Crosses

5/5 Right Cross

1. Slip the next five stitches to a cable needle and hold at the back of the work.

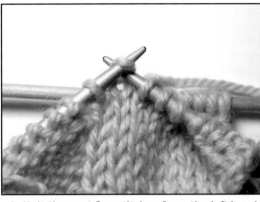

2. Knit the next five stitches from the left-hand needle.

3. Knit the five stitches from the cable needle.

5/5 Left Cross

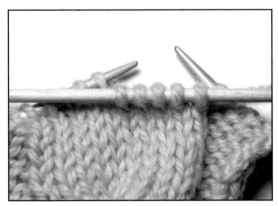

1. Slip the next five stitches to a cable needle and hold at the front of the work.

2. Knit the next five stitches from the left-hand needle.

3. Knit the five stitches from the cable needle.

Pattern 8.5: Another good cable stitch pattern to pair with its bulky counterparts, this is a supersized version of the Aran Honeycomb pattern.

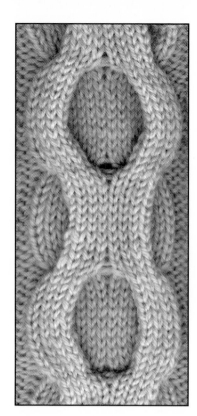

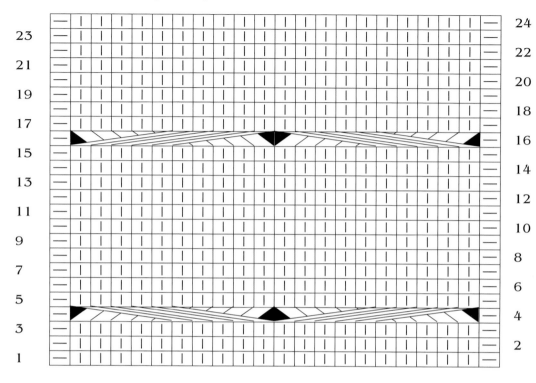

Panel of 22 stitches

Row 1 and all other WS rows: K1, p20, k1
Rows 2, 6, 8, 10, 12, 14, 18, 20, 22 and 24: P1, k20, p1
Row 4: P1, 5/5 RC, 5/5 LC, p1
Row 16: P1, 5/5 LC, 5/5 RC, p1

6/6 Knit Crosses

6/6 Right Cross

1. Slip the next six stitches to a cable needle and hold at the back of the work.

2. Knit the next six stitches from the left-hand needle.

3. Knit the six stitches from the cable needle.

6/6 Left Cross

1. Slip the next six stitches to a cable needle and hold at the front of the work.

2. Knit the next six stitches from the left-hand needle.

3. Knit the six stitches from the cable needle.

Pattern 8.6: Because of their tendency to distort fabric laterally, larger crosses such as 6/6 right and left crosses just aren't widely used. Here is one basic cable which should be familiar by now—the rope cable.

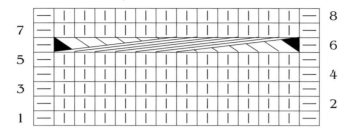

Panel of 14 stitches

Row 1 and all other WS rows: K1, p12, k1
Rows 2, 4 and 8: P1, k12, p1
Row 6: P1, 6/6 RC, p1

Pattern 8.7: This nautical-looking cable is the perfect choice for that custom Aran design. Pair it with other bold cables for something stunning.

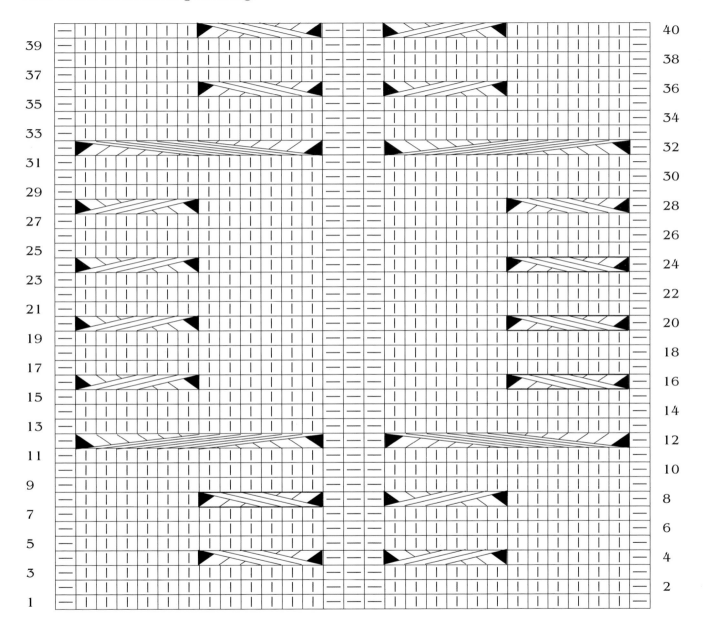

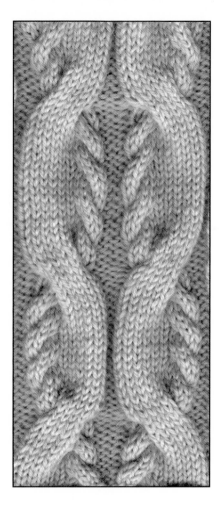

Panel of 29 stitches

Row 1 and all other WS rows: K1, p12, k3, p12, k1
Rows 2, 6, 10, 14, 18, 22, 26, 30, 34 and 38: P1, k12, p3, k12, p1
Rows 4, 8, 36 and 40: P1, k6, 3/3 RC, p3, 3/3 LC, k6, p1
Row 12: P1, 6/6 LC, p3, 6/6 RC, p1
Rows 16, 20, 24 and 28: P1, 3/3 LC, k6, p3, k6, 3/3 RC, p1
Row 32: P1, 6/6 RC, p3, 6/6 LC, p1

Chapter 9

Unique Techniques

This group of cables gets its own chapter because the techniques involved in crossing stitches are not the ones normally associated with cables and twists. The result is the same—stitches moved—but the methods for making that happen are interesting and unusual.

Woven Cables:

This is one of my favorite cables. I think it has a very contemporary look. It's quite easy to work once you understand the mechanism behind it. Half the stitches of the cable are placed on a cable needle and held at either the back or front of the work. Then, instead of knitting all the stitches from the left-hand needle followed by all the stitches from the cable needle, the stitches are knitted alternately—first one from the left-hand needle, then one from the cable needle, then one from the left-hand needle, *etc.* It is shown here over ten stitches, but could be worked over any even number of stitches.

Woven Right Cross

1. Place half the stitches on a cable needle and hold at the back of the work.

2. Knit the next stitch from the left-hand needle.

3. Knit the next stitch from the cable needle. Alternate steps 2 and 3 until all stitches of the cable have been worked.

Woven Left Cross

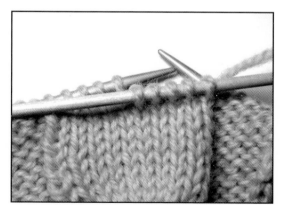

1. Slip half the stitches to a cable needle and hold at the front of the work.

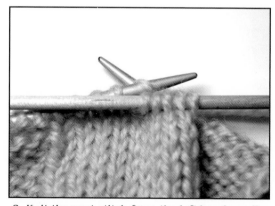

2. Knit the next stitch from the left-hand needle.

3. Knit the next stitch from the cable needle. Alternate steps 2 and 3 until all stitches of the cable have been worked.

Pattern 9.1: The rope cable version of a woven cable is shown here, but it can also be worked as a wave cable, alternating the direction of the crosses.

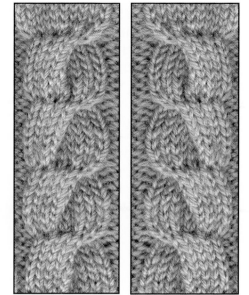

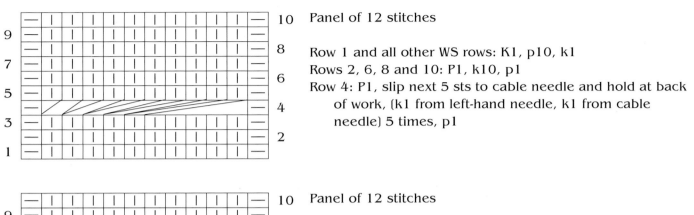

Panel of 12 stitches

Row 1 and all other WS rows: K1, p10, k1
Rows 2, 6, 8 and 10: P1, k10, p1
Row 4: P1, slip next 5 sts to cable needle and hold at back of work, (k1 from left-hand needle, k1 from cable needle) 5 times, p1

Panel of 12 stitches

Row 1 and all other WS rows: K1, p10, k1
Rows 2, 6, 8 and 10: P1, k10, p1
Row 4: P1, slip next 5 sts to cable needle and hold at front of work, (k1 from left-hand needle, k1 from cable needle) 5 times, p1

Slip next 5 sts to cable needle and hold at back of work, (k1 from left-hand needle, k1 from cable needle) 5 times

Slip next 5 sts to cable needle and hold at front of work, (k1 from left-hand needle, k1 from cable needle) 5 times

180-Degree Turned Cables: Try these cables once, for the sheer fun of it. The stitches in these cables do not exchange places with each other. Rather, the entire group of cable stitches is placed on a cable needle, and the needle rotated 180 degrees (either left or right, depending upon the desired result). The stitches are knitted off the turned cable needle.

180-Degree Right Turn

1. Slip all the stitches to a cable needle.

2. Rotate the cable needle 180 degrees to the right (the end is marked).

3. Knit the stitches from the cable needle in the turned position.

180-Degree Left Turn

1. Slip all the stitches to a cable needle.

2. Rotate the cable needle 180 degrees to the left (the end is marked).

3. Knit the stitches from the cable needle in the turned position.

Pattern 9.2: Always turning the cable needle in the same direction—either left or right—creates a rope cable. Alternate the direction of the turns and form a wave cable, instead.

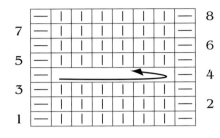

Panel of 8 stitches

Row 1 and all other WS rows: K1, p6, k1
Rows 2, 6 and 8: P1, k6, p1
Row 4: P1, place next 6 stitches on cable needle and rotate them 180 degrees to the right, then k6 from cable needle, p1

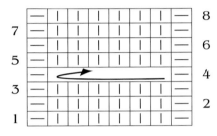

Panel of 8 stitches

Row 1 and all other WS rows: K1, p6, k1
Rows 2, 6 and 8: P1, k6, p1
Row 4: P1, place next 6 stitches on cable needle and rotate them 180 degrees to the left, then k6 from cable needle, p1

 Place next 6 stitches on cable needle and rotate them 180 degrees to the right, then k6 from cable needle

 Place next 6 stitches on cable needle and rotate them 180 degrees to the left, then k6 from cable needle

Gordion Knots: These crosses are similar to the 2/2/2 crosses found in Chapter 6. However, in these versions, the two central purl stitches are in front of the two two-stitch knit ribs.

Gordion Knot Right

1. Slip the next two stitches to a cable needle and hold at the back of the work. Slip the following two stitches to a cable needle and hold at the front of the work.

2. Knit the next two stitches from the left-hand needle.

3. Purl the two stitches from the front cable needle.

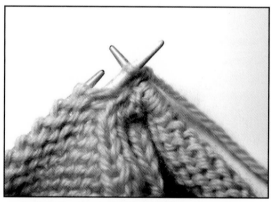

4. Knit the two stitches from the back cable needle.

1. Slip the next four stitches to a cable needle and hold at the front of the work.

2. Knit the next two stitches from the left-hand needle.

3. Slip the two left-most stitches from the cable needle back to the left-hand needle, pass the cable needle to the back of the work, then purl the two stitches from the left-hand needle.

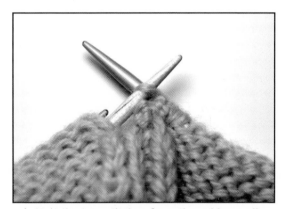

4. Knit the two stitches from the cable needle.

Gordion Knot Left

Pattern 9.3: This simple cable is another great alternative to the standard four-stitch rope cable.

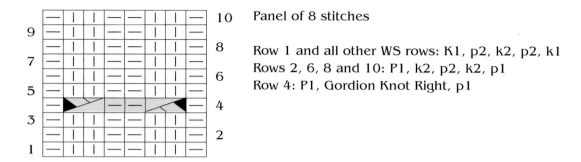

10 Panel of 8 stitches

Row 1 and all other WS rows: K1, p2, k2, p2, k1
Rows 2, 6, 8 and 10: P1, k2, p2, k2, p1
Row 4: P1, Gordion Knot Right, p1

 Gordion Knot Right: Slip next 2 sts to cable needle and hold at back of work, slip next 2 sts to cable needle and hold at front of work, k2, then p2 from front cable needle, k2 from back cable needle

208

3-2-1 Twists: In this technique, a group of three stitches is twisted by knitting the third stitch on the left-hand needle, then the second stitch on the left-hand needle, and finally the first stitch—and all three are dropped from the left-hand needle simultaneously. It's a subtle maneuver which appears similar to a traditional 1/3 right cross, but is easier to work.

3-2-1 Twist

1. Bring the right-hand needle in front and knit the third stitch on the left-hand needle. Do not drop it off the needle.

2. Knit the second stitch on the left-hand needle. Do not drop it off the needle.

3. Knit the first stitch on the needle. Drop all three stitches from the left-hand needle.

Pattern 9.4: This simple twist pattern is a useful accent or small divider between larger patterns.

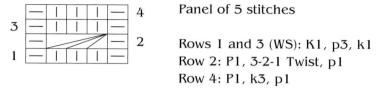

Panel of 5 stitches

Rows 1 and 3 (WS): K1, p3, k1
Row 2: P1, 3-2-1 Twist, p1
Row 4: P1, k3, p1

 3-2-1 Twist: Bring the right-hand needle in front and knit into the third, then the second, then the first stitch on the left-hand needle, dropping them all from the left-hand needle at the same time.

Chapter 10

Designing Original Cable Patterns

Designing original stitch patterns is much like arranging or composing music. Once the fundamentals of music theory and playing have been mastered, the musician is able to create novel arrangements of existing tunes, or compose totally original musical pieces. Designing original stitch patterns is a very similar process. As you worked your way through the book to this point, I hope you began to see the relationships between knit and purl stitches as they form cables. As you become more and more familiar with cables, designing original cable stitch patterns becomes easier—and even great fun! In this chapter, I share with you two techniques for creating new cable stitch patterns: altering existing patterns or charting new ones from scratch.

1. Adapt or change an existing stitch pattern: This is the easiest way to begin designing original stitch patterns. Some might argue that tweaking an existing pattern is not the same as creating a totally original one, but a series of changes can alter the original pattern beyond recognition, thus creating something new. Sometimes merely swapping out one element of a cable pattern for another creates a completely new cable stitch. When I encounter a stitch pattern for the first time, I like to break it down into its component parts:

How many stitches in the multiple?
How many rows in the repeat?
What kind of crosses make up the cable?
Are the crosses tight, loose, simple or complex?
Are there other elements, such a filler stitches, making up the stitch pattern?

This kind of quick analysis leads to ideas about what elements can be changed. Let's take a look at some examples:

Example 1: One evening, while flipping through *Vogue Knitting Stitchionary Volume 2: Cables*, I came across Pattern 120: Braid Panels. I was intrigued, so I swatched it. Five stitches of plain stockinette alternate with a three-stitch braid cable flanked on each side by a single column of garter stitch, forming a stitch pattern with a multiple of 10 stitches + 2 and a row repeat of 40 rows. After the first 20 rows,

the cable and stockinette sections change places. I liked the stitch pattern as presented in the book, especially the bit of added texture provided by the garter stitch columns. Looking at the chart, though, I could see that the basic structure of the stitch pattern would lend itself well to some changes.

Here is the original pattern:

Multiple of 10 stitches + 2

Row 1 and all other WS rows: K1, purl to last st, k1

Rows 2, 6, 10, 14 and 18: P1, *k5, p1, 1/1 RC, k1, p1; rep from *, end p1

Rows 4, 8, 12, 16 and 20: P1, *k5, p1, k1, 1/1 LC, p1; rep from *, end p1

Rows 22, 26, 30, 34 and 38: P1, *p1, 1/1 RC, k1, p1, k5; rep from *, end p1

Rows 24, 28, 32, 36 and 40: P1, *p1, k1, 1/1 LC, p1, k5; rep from *, end p1

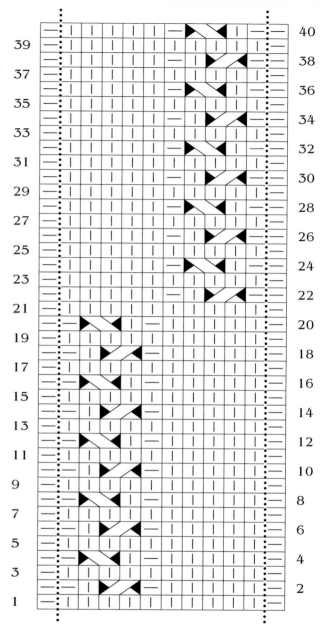

Thus began a series of modifications. First, I wondered how the original stitch pattern would look as a ribbing pattern, instead of a staggered one. I liked this stitch pattern a lot and almost stopped here, planning to use this stitch pattern in a pullover. I set that idea aside, though, and continued to experiment.

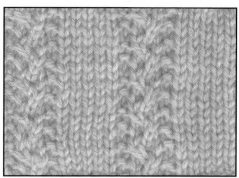

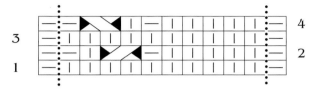

Multiple of 10 stitches + 2

Rows 1 and 3 (WS): K1, purl to last st, k1
Row 2: P1, *k5, p1, 1/1 RC, k1, p1; rep from *, end p1
Row 4: P1, *k5, p1, k1, 1/1 LC, p1; rep from *, end p1

I was curious to see what the stitch pattern would look like with something other than a braid at the center. What about a rope cable? The rope cable is visually heavier than the braid cable and I predicted (correctly) that the stitch pattern would be a bit bolder. Because the rope cable is composed of four stitches, not three as in the original braid cable, I increased the number of stockinette stitches between the cables from five to six (to balance the combination of the cable itself plus its flanking garter-stitch columns). The stitch pattern thus became a multiple of 12 stitches + 2. Although it is shown here in a ribbed version, it would work equally well in a staggered version.

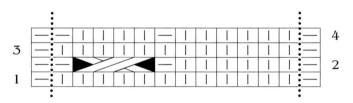

Multiple of 12 stitches + 2

Rows 1 and 3 (WS): K1, purl to last st, k1
Row 2: P1, *k6, p1, 2/2 RC, p1; rep from *, end p1
Row 4: P1, *k6, p1, k4, p1; rep from *, end p1

Next, I thought about what other three-, four-, and even five-stitch cables might work instead of the rope cable. Suppose I swapped the rope cable with a small honeycomb cable? Wow, I really liked that one.

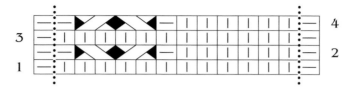

Multiple of 12 stitches + 2

Row 1 and all other WS rows: K1, purl to last st, k1
Row 2: P1, *k6, p1, 1/1 RC, 1/1 LC, p1; rep from *, end p1
Row 4: P1, *k6, p1, 1/1 LC, 1/1 RC, p1; rep from *, end p1

After carrying the swatch around with me for a few days and getting to know it, I realized that two repeats of the small honeycomb pattern looked very much like a figure-eight pattern. Aha! What if I isolated that figure-eight pattern, staggering it once again? The result? A stitch pattern which evolved from—but looks nothing like—the original pattern from *Vogue Stitchionary Volume 2: Cables*.

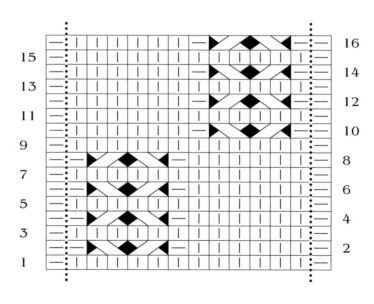

Multiple of 12 stitches + 2

Row 1 and all other WS rows: K1, purl to last st, end k1
Rows 2 and 6: P1, *k6, p1, 1/1 RC, 1/1 LC, p1; rep from *, end p1
Rows 4 and 8: P1, *k6, p1, 1/1 LC, 1/1 RC, p1; rep from *, end p1
Rows 10 and 14: P1, *p1, 1/1 RC, 1/1 LC, p1, k6; rep from *, end p1
Rows 12 and 16: P1, *p1, 1/1 LC, 1/1 RC, p1, k6; rep from *, end p1

Example 2: Here, I've taken a well-known cable stitch pattern (it's often referred to as "Saxon Braid") and swapped out the cable crosses to create a new stitch pattern. First, let's look at the original pattern:

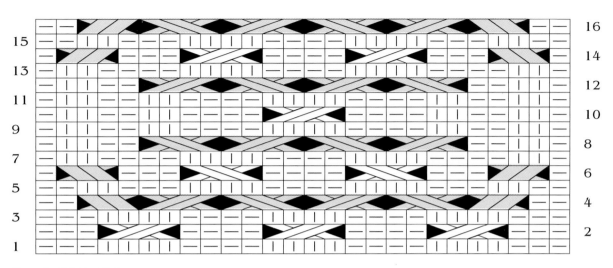

Panel of 26 stitches

Rows 1 and 3 (WS): K3, (p4, k4) twice, p4, k3
Row 2: P3, (2/2 RC, p4) twice, 2/2 RC, p3
Row 4: P2, 2/1 RPC, (2/2 LPC, 2/2 RPC) twice, 2/1 LPC, p2
Rows 5 and 15: K2, p2, k3, p4, k4, p4, k3, p2, k2
Row 6: P1, 2/1 RPC, p3, 2/2 LC, p4, 2/2 LC, p3, 2/1 LPC, p1
Rows 7 and 13: K1, p2, (k4, p4) twice, k4, p2, k1
Row 8: P1, k2, p2, (2/2 RPC, 2/2 LPC) twice, p2, k2, p1
Rows 9 and 11: K1, p2, k2, p2, k4, p4, k4, p2, k2, p2, k1
Row 10: P1, k2, p2, k2, p4, 2/2 RC, p4, k2, p2, k2, p1
Row 12: P1, k2, p2, (2/2 LPC, 2/2 RPC) twice, p2, k2, p1
Row 14: P1, 2/1 LPC, p3, 2/2 RC, p4, 2/2 RC, p3, 2/1 RPC, p1
Row 16: P2, 2/1 LPC, (2/2 RPC, 2/2 LPC) twice, 2/1 RPC, p2

The original stitch pattern consists of a combination of 2/2 knit crosses, 2/2 purl crosses, and 2/1 purl crosses. What would happen if 2/1 purl crosses were substituted for the 2/2 purl crosses on rows 4, 8, 12 and 16? All other crosses remain unchanged.

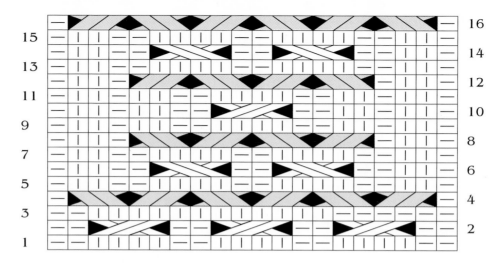

Panel of 20 stitches

Rows 1 and 3 (WS): K2, (p4, k2) three times
Row 2: P2, (2/2 RC, p2) three times
Row 4: P1, (2/1 RPC, (2/1 LPC) three times, p1
Rows 5, 7, 13 and 15: K1, p2, (k2, p4) twice, k2, p2, k1
Rows 6 and 14: P1, K2, (p2, 2/2 LC) twice, p2, k2, p1
Row 8: P1, k2, p1, (2/1 RPC, 2/1 LPC) twice, p1, k2, p1
Rows 9 and 11: K1, p2, k1, p2, k2, p4, k2, p2, k1, p2, k1
Row 10: (P1, k2) twice, p2, 2/2 RC, p2, (k2, p1) twice
Row 12: P1, k2, p1, (2/1 LPC, 2/1 RPC) twice, p1, k2, p1
Row 16: P1, (2/1 RPC, 2/1 LPC) three times, p1

Now, the panel is 20 stitches wide instead of 26, and the cable crosses on rows 6 and 14 are separated by only two purl stitches instead of four. The whole effect is of a much more laterally compressed cable, but one that still resembles the original Saxon Braid. Note that the number of rows in the pattern has not changed.

Example 3: Another change I'll often make is to substitute two-stitch cable ribs for a pattern featuring three-stitch cable ribs. Many of the cable patterns in Barbara Walker's stitch dictionaries are simply too bold and overwhelming for use in a design, and they often require liberal use of increases and decreases to account for cable splay. Substituting smaller cable crosses and two-stitch ribs makes these cables more suitable for designs where bold cables aren't desired, and reduces cable splay.

This example is the "Looping Wave" pattern from Barbara Walker's *Charted Knitting Designs*.

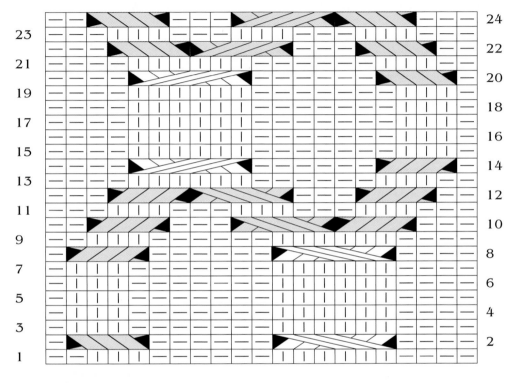

Panel of 21 stitches

Rows 1 and 9 (WS): K2, p3, k6, p6, k4
Row 2: P4, 3/3 LC, p6, 3/1 LPC, p1
Rows 3, 5 and 7: K1, p3, k7, p6, k4
Rows 4 and 6: P4, k6, p7, k3, p1
Row 8: P4, 3/3 LC, p6, 3/1 RPC, p1
Row 10: P3, 3/1 RPC, 3/2 LPC, p3, 3/1 RPC, p2
Rows 11 and 23: (K3, p3) three times, k3
Row 12: P2, 3/1 RPC, p3, 3/2 LPC, 3/1 RPC, p3

Rows 13 and 21: K4, p6, k6, p3, k2
Row 14: P1, 3/1 RPC, p6, 3/3 RC, p4
Rows 15, 17 and 19: K4, p6, k7, p3, k1
Rows 16 and 18: P1, k3, p7, k6, p4
Row 20: P1, 3/1 LPC, p6, 3/3 RC, p4
Row 22: P2, 3/1 LPC, p3, 3/2 RPC, 3/1 LPC, p3
Row 24: P3, 3/1 LPC, 3/2 RPC, p3, 3/1 LPC, p2

This is the revised chart and pattern. Note that the three-stitch cable ribs have been changed to two-stitch ribs, and the crosses adjusted accordingly. Because the 3/3 crosses are now 2/2 crosses, they require only three intervening plain rows (rows 3-5 and 13-15) instead of five as in the original pattern. This shortens the overall row repeat by four rows.

Note, too, that there remain seven purl stitches between the main trunk of the cable and the loop which swings outward (rows 3-5 and 13-15 again); this is the same number as in the original pattern. However, these seven stitches are less overwhelmed by the cable ribs in this version. In fact, this change provides an opportunity to fill that plain space with some kind of filler stitch.

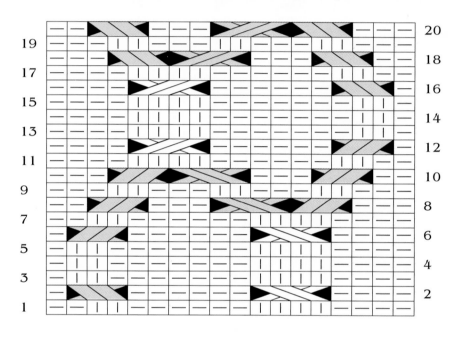

Panel of 18 stitches

Rows 1 and 7 (WS): K2, p2, k6, p4, k4
Row 2: P4, 2/2 LC, p6, 2/1 LPC, p1
Rows 3 and 5: K1, p2, k7, p4, k4
Row 4: P4, k4, p7, k2, p1
Row 6: P4, 2/2 LC, p6, 2/1 RPC, p1
Row 8: P3, 2/1 RPC, 2/2 LPC, p3, 2/1 RPC, p2
Rows 9 and 19: (K3, p2) three times, k3
Row 10: P2, 2/1 RPC, p3, 2/2 LPC, 2/1 RPC, p3
Rows 11 and 17: K4, p4, k6, p2, k2

Row 12: P1, 2/1 RPC, p6, 2/2 RC, p4
Rows 13 and 15: K4, p4, k7, p2, k1
Row 14: P1, k2, p7, k4, p4
Row 16: P1, 2/1 LPC, p6, 2/2 RC, p4
Row 18: P2, 2/1 LPC, p3, 2/2 RPC, 2/1 LPC, p3
Row 20: P3, 2/1 LPC, 2/2 RPC, p3, 2/1 LPC, p2

2. Chart out a new stitch pattern from scratch: This is (I think) a bit more challenging exercise than the previous method. However, if you're willing to do a little sketching and a lot of swatching, you may be richly rewarded!

It helps to become familiar with the various cable crosses and the angles they form. Let's look at 2/1, 2/2, and 2/3 right crosses:

   2/1 right cross

   2/2 right cross

   2/3 right cross

You are welcome to knit some of these cables, then get out a protractor and measure the angles. For purposes of discussion, however, let's assume the following:

    1. The 2/1 right cross leans at an angle of 60 degrees.
    2. The 2/2 right cross leans at an angle of 45 degrees.
    3. The 2/3 right cross leans at an angle of 30 degrees.

Knowing the angles formed by the various cable crosses makes it easier to choose the correct cross for a given situation.

Here is where you get to do a bit of doodling. Get a sharp pencil (and an eraser) and a piece of paper and let your imagination go. Do you see an angular cable with lots of sharp turns, or do you see a free-flowing, curvy one? Or a combination of the two? The kind of lines making up that cable will determine what crosses you choose:

• Straight lines are composed of crosses of the same type or "angle"—all 2/2 crosses, for example.

• Curvy lines are composed of a mix of crosses—for example, 2/1, 2/2, *and* 2/3.

• Sharp angles are where a straight line abruptly changes direction—from a 2/2 right cross to a 2/2 left cross.

• Soft angles have more non-cabling rows between the change in direction.

I will caution you that it's easy to put a lot of work into creating what you think is an "original" cable, only to crack open the nearest stitch dictionary and find that very same pattern! We're all influenced subconsciously by what we have seen. Nevertheless, practicing increases the odds that you *will* create a completely original cable pattern.

Example 1: I drew a simple cable consisting of two parallel lines with cable ribs traveling between them (note that my drawing skills are nothing to write home about, so don't be afraid to sketch out your ideas!). The lines connecting the parallel, vertical ribs lean at about 45 degrees, so 2/2 right purl crosses were the natural choice. I added some 2/2 right crosses where the lines come together and wrap around each other and voila!—a stitch pattern is born.

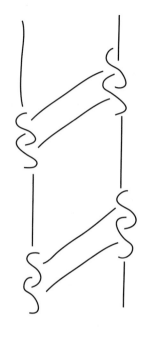 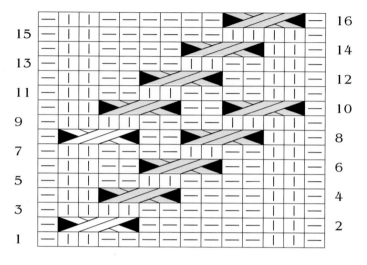

Panel of 14 stitches

Row 1 (WS): K1, p2, k8, p2, k1
Row 2: P1, k2, p6, 2/2 RC, p1
Row 3: K1, p4, k6, p2, k1
Row 4: P1, k2, p4, 2/2 RPC, k2, p1
Row 5: K1, p2, k2, p2, k4, p2, k1
Row 6: P1, k2, p2, 2/2 RPC, p2, k2, p1
Row 7: K1, p2, k4, p2, k2, p2, k1
Row 8: P1, k2, 2/2 RPC, p2, 2/2 RC, p1
Row 9: K1, p4, k4, p4, k1
Row 10: P1, 2/2 RPC, p2, 2/2 RPC, k2, p1
Row 11: K1, p2, k2, p2, k4, p2, k1
Row 12: P1, k2, p2, 2/2 RPC, p2, k2, p1
Row 13: K1, p2, k4, p2, k2, p2, k1
Row 14: P1, k2, 2/2 RPC, p4, k2, p1
Row 15: K1, p2, k6, p4, k1
Row 16: P1, 2/2 RPC, p6, k2, p1

Example 2: Here I started with three rope cables, then spun them out into their component two-stitch ribs that traveled in something of a butterfly shape before coming back to meet. Just looking at the butterfly section gave me a sense of a braid pattern similar to that in pattern 4.14 variation #2, so I actually began charting at the center of the butterfly section, working my way out from there. That's an important point that makes charting original stitch patterns much easier: it's not necessary to begin charting from the bottom and working up. Sometimes a chart is easier to create when starting with the known part and working out (or in) to the unknown. And keep in mind that it might take several swatches—with adjustments to the crosses, if necessary—to produce a final version.

As with the previous example, there are lots of 45-degree angles in this pattern; however, there are also some 60-degree angles for which the 2/1 crosses were the perfect fit.

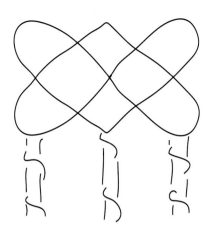

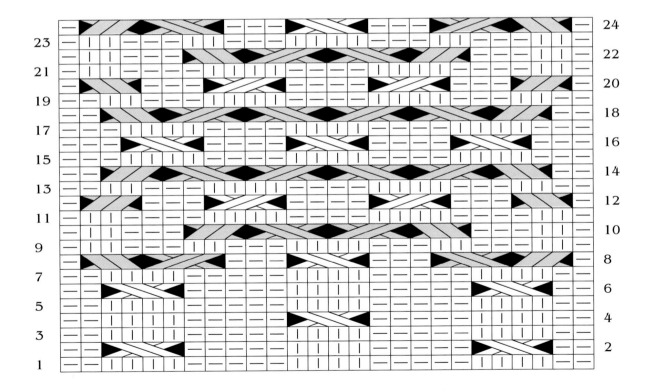

Panel of 26 stitches

Rows 1, 3, 5 and 7 (WS): K2, (p4, k5) twice, p4, k2
Rows 2 and 6: P2, 2/2 LC, p5, k4, p5, 2/2 LC, p2
Row 4: P2, k4, p5, 2/2 LC, p5, k4, p2
Row 8: P1, 2/1 RPC, 2/2 LPC, p3, 2/2 LC, p3, 2/2 RPC, 2/1 LPC, p1
Rows 9 and 23: K1, (p2, k3) twice, p4, (k3, p2) twice, k1
Row 10: P1, k2, p3, 2/1 LPC, 2/2 RPC, 2/2 LPC, 2/1 RPC, p3, k2, p1
Rows 11 and 21: K1, p2, (k4, p4) twice, k4, p2, k1
Row 12: P1, 2/1 LPC, p3, 2/2 RC, p4, 2/2 RC, p3, 2/1 RPC, p1
Rows 13 and 19: K2, p2, k3, p4, k4, p4, k3, p2, k2
Row 14: P2, 2/1 LPC, (2/2 RPC, 2/2 LPC) twice, 2/1 RPC, p2
Rows 15 and 17: K3, (p4, k4) twice, p4, k3
Row 16: P3, (2/2 LC, p4) twice, 2/2 LC, p3
Row 18: P2, 2/1 RPC, (2/2 LPC, 2/2 RPC) twice, 2/1 LPC, p2
Row 20: P1, 2/1 RPC, p3, 2/2 RC, p4, 2/2 RC, p3, 2/1 LPC, p1
Row 22: P1, k2, p3, 2/1 RPC, 2/2 LPC, 2/2 RPC, 2/1 LPC, p3, k2, p1
Row 24: P1, 2/1 LPC, 2/2 RPC, p3, 2/2 LC, p3, 2/2 LPC, 2/1 RPC, p1

Whatever approach you might take, designing original cable stitch patterns—or even adapting existing ones—is a fun way to expand your cabling abilities.

Bibliography

This is a list of the stitch dictionaries I used as resources when preparing this book. It is by no means an exhaustive list, but represents the ones to which I refer most often.

Abbey, Barbara. *The Complete Book of Knitting*. New York, NY: Viking Press, Inc., 1971.

Big Book of Knitting Stitch Patterns. New York, NY: Sterling Publishing Co., 2004.

Harmony Guides. Volume 2, *450 Knitting Stitches*. New York, NY: Collins & Brown, Ltd., 1998.

Harmony Guides. Volume 3, *440 More Knitting Stitches*. New York, NY: Collins & Brown, Ltd., 1998.

Harmony Guides. Volume 4, *250 Creative Knitting Stitches*. New York, NY: Collins & Brown, Ltd., 1998.

Harmony Guides. Volume 5, *220 Aran Stitches and Patterns*. New York, NY: Collins & Brown, Ltd., 1998.

Klöpper, Gisela. *Beautiful Knitting Patterns.* New York, NY: Sterling Publishing Co., 2003.

Leapman, Melissa. *Cables Untangled*. New York, NY: Potter Craft, 2006.

Maloney, Annie. *The Cable Knitting Handbook*. Belleville, ON: Self-Published, 2004.

Matthews, Anne. *Vogue Dictionary of Knitting Stitches*. New York, NY: Condé Nast Publications, Ltd., 1984.

Mon Tricot: 1800 Patterns. Paris: Cie Française d'Éditions Gastronomiques, 1989.

Reader's Digest, *The Ultimate Sourcebook of Knitting and Crochet Stitches*. Pleasantville, NY: Collins & Brown, Ltd., 2003.

Stanfield, Lesley, and Melody Griffiths. *The Encyclopedia of Knitting*. London: Quarto Publishing, 2000.

Vogue Stitchionary Volume 1: Knit & Purl. Carla Scott. New York, NY: Sixth & Spring Books, 2005.

Vogue Stitchionary Volume 2: Cables. Carla Scott. New York, NY: Sixth & Spring Books, 2005.

Walker, Barbara. *A Treasury of Knitting Patterns*. Pittsville, WI: Schoolhouse Press, 1998.

Walker, Barbara. *A Second Treasury of Knitting Patterns*. Pittsville, WI: Schoolhouse Press, 1998.

Walker, Barbara. *Charted Knitting Designs: A Third Treasury of Knitting Patterns*. Pittsville, WI: Schoolhouse Press, 1998.

Walker, Barbara. *A Fourth Treasury of Knitting Patterns*. Pittsville, WI: Schoolhouse Press, 2001.

Webb, Mary. *Knitting Stitches*. Buffalo, NY: Firefly Books, 2006.

I also have seven Japanese knitting stitch books to which I refer often. I cannot translate the publishing information, so I have listed them here with their ISBN numbers.

1000 Knitting Patterns Book, ISBN 4-529-02141-4

500 Knitting Patterns, ISBN 4-529-01588-2

100 Aran Patterns, ISBN 4-529-02293-5

Knitting Patterns Book, 300 ISBN 4-529-04172-7

Knitting Patterns, 300 ISBN 4-529-02071-1

250 Knitting Patterns, ISBN 4-529-04228-6

250 Knitting Patterns Book, ISBN 4-529-04176-X

Index

angles, 219–221

B

basketweave patterns, 87
Bavarian stitch patterns, 58–59
bias, 13
birds in flight pattern, 77
bobbles, 125
braid patterns, 74–75, 88, 103–107, 114–115, 144, 157, 188, 192, 212, 215–216
branching pattern, 67, 79, 128

C

cable needles, 14
cable splay, 18–19, 217
cabling without a cable needle, 14–15, 33
chain patterns, 177
Charted Knitting Designs (Walker), 18, 85
charting new patterns, 219–222
charts, 17–18

D

designing original cable patterns, 211–222
    adapting existing cable patterns, 211–218
    charting new patterns, 219–222
diamond patterns, 40, 52–55, 55, 67, 73, 102, 113, 154–155, 184–185

E

eight-stitch crosses, 189–200
    4/4 crosses, 190–192
    symbols for, 28

F

filler stitch, 51, 54, 95, 125, 138, 184–185
Five-Fold Aran Braid, 144
five-stitch crosses, 123–149
    1/3/1 knit crosses, 136–138
    2/1/2 knit crosses, 139–141

2/1/2 purl crosses, 142–145
2/3 knit crosses, 124–125
2/3 purl crosses, 126–128
3/2 knit crosses, 129–132
3/2 purl crosses, 133–135
4/1 knit crosses, 146
4/1 purl crosses, 147–149
symbols for, 25–26
floral-themed patterns, 64
four-stitch crosses, 83–121
    1/2/1 knit crosses, 116–118
    1/2/1 purl crosses, 119–121
    1/3 knit crosses, 84–85
    1/3 purl crosses, 85
    2/2 crosses, 98–107
    2/2 knit crosses, 86–97
    3/1 knit crosses, 108–109
    3/1 purl crosses, 110–115
    symbols for, 24–25

G

Gordian knot, 206–208
graph paper, 18

H

half-drop formation, 54, 55
Harmony series, 16
herringbone-style pattern, 38
honeycomb cable, 41, 42, 94–95, 141, 196, 214
horseshoe-style cable, 63, 85, 92, 160
hourglass patterns, 47, 48, 71

K

key to charts, 22–29
    two-stitch crosses, symbols for, 22–23
    three-stitch crosses, symbols for, 23–24
    four-stitch crosses, symbols for, 24–25
    five-stitch crosses, symbols for, 25–26
    six-stitch crosses, symbols for, 26–28

1/1/1 crosses, 80–82
1/1/1 knit crosses, 76–77
1/1/1 reverse knit cross, 78–79
1/2 knit crosses, 62–63
1/2 purl crosses, 64–65
2/1 knit crosses, 66–67
2/1 purl crosses, 68–75
symbols for, 23–24
traveling line, 111, 114, 135
Treasury of Knitting Patterns, A (Walker), 132
trellis patterns, 40, 49–52, 72, 75, 82, 101, 102, 121
trim pattern, 38
twelve-stitch crosses
6/6 knit crosses, 197–200
symbols for, 29
twists
1/1 all-purl crosses, twist versions, 56–57
1/1 knit crosses, twist versions, 34–35
1/1 purl crosses, twist versions, 45
twists, cables vs., 31–32
two-stitch crosses, 31–59
1/1 all-purl crosses, twist versions, 56–57
1/1 crosses, every row, 58–59
1/1 knit crosses, cable versions, 33
1/1 knit crosses, twist versions, 34–35
1/1 purl crosses, 46–55
1/1 purl crosses, cable versions, 44
1/1 purl crosses, twist versions, 45
symbols for, 22–23

U

uneven cable, 194
unusual techniques, 201–209

V

Vogue Knitting Stitchionary Volume 2: Cables,
211, 214
V-shaped cable, 109, 112

W

Walker, Barbara, 16, 18, 34, 85, 132, 217
wave patterns, 91, 125, 159, 191, 203
woolen-spun yarns, 11–13
worsted-spun yarns, 11–13
woven cables, 202–203

X

XO patterns, 96
XRX, Inc., 22
X-shape pattern, 37

Y

yarn construction, 11–13

Z

zig-zagging lines, 39, 40, 46–49, 69, 71, 99–101, 134–135, 145, 148–149. See also diamond patterns; trellis patterns